The Cracked Pot

BI44-11

The
Cracked Pot

THE STATE OF TODAY'S
ANGLICAN PARISH CLERGY

YVONNE WARREN

**kevin
mayhew**

First published in 2002 by
KEVIN MAYHEW LTD
Buxhall, Stowmarket, Suffolk IP14 3BW
E-mail: info@kevinmayhewltd.com

9 8 7 6 5 4 3 2 1 0

ISBN 1 84003 851 9
Catalogue No. 1500477

Cover design by Angela Selfe
Typeset by Louise Selfe

Printed and bound in Great Britain

The Church in the twenty-first century is experiencing a cataclysmic time of change. This has affected patterns of ministry more than most, and many clergy are feeling the impact of this, not just in terms of increased workload, but in their sense of frustration and feeling of increasing irrelevance in a largely secularised society. *The Cracked Pot* investigates how Anglican clergy are experiencing and coping with the changes both within the Church and in the world around.

Through extensive research among the clergy it looks at:

- how the clergy understand their calling and vocation
- their attitudes to authority
- their understanding of priesthood
- their home and family life
- how they exercise leadership
- the impact on their health, emotional and spiritual as well as physical
- pastoral care for the clergy

Dr Yvonne Warren is a Psychotherapist and Marital Therapist, but writes from her own long experience as a clergy spouse as well as from her research and work. She is unafraid to confront tough issues, but uses the image of *The Cracked Pot* not only to describe the painful realities, but also to offer the hope that through the cracks and damage caused in ministry the light of Christ will shine more brightly. This book is an essential read for any concerned about issues of ministry and care of the clergy.

STUART THOMAS

Acknowledgements

The publishers wish to express their gratitude to the following for permission to include copyright material in this book:

Blackwell Publishers, 108 Cowley Road, Oxford, OX4 1JF for the extracts from *Religion in Britain since 1945* by G. Davie (1994).

Church House Publishing, Church House, Great Smith Street, London, SW1P 3NZ, for the extracts from *The Alternative Service Book* 1980 © The Central Board of Finance of the Church of England, 1980; The Archbishops' Council, 1999.

Constable & Robinson Ltd, 3 The Lanchesters, 162 Fulham Palace Road, London, W6 9ER, for the extracts from *One Flesh Separate Persons* by A. C. R. Skynner (1976).

Gracewing Publishing, 2 Southern Avenue, Leominster, Herefordshire, HR6 0QF, for the extract from *Psychological Perspectives on Christian Ministry* by C. J. Francis and S. H. Jones (1996).

Sweet & Maxwell Ltd, Cheriton House, North Way, Andover, Hampshire, SP10 5BE for the extracts from *Ecclesiastical Law Handbook* by Lynne Leeder (1977).

Dr Fraser Watts and Professor J. M. G.Williams for the extracts from *The Psychology of Religious Knowing* by F. Watts and M. Williams (Cambridge University Press, 1988).

Yale University Press, 302 Temple Street, New Haven, CT 06511, USA for the extracts from *Psychoanalysis and Religious Experience* by W. W. Meissner (1984).

Every effort has been made to trace the owners of copyright material and we hope that no copyright has been infringed. Pardon is sought and apology made if the contrary be the case, and a correction will be made in any reprint of this book.

Contents

Introduction   9

Chapter 1: The cracks appear
The pressure of change   19

Chapter 2: A holy calling
Why they were ordained   31

Chapter 3: I did it my way
Attitudes to authority   49

Chapter 4: To be or not to be . . .
What it means to be a priest   72

Chapter 5: Knowing me, knowing you
Home life, family and friends   96

Chapter 6: In the driving seat
Leader within the parish   125

Chapter 7: The cracked pot
Emotional and spiritual health   156

Chapter 8: Who cares for the carers?
Pastors for the clergy   197

Chapter 9: The end?
Treasures in jars of clay   211

Appendix 1   219

Appendix 2   223

Appendix 3   225

Appendix 4   229

Appendix 5   230

Appendix 6   231

Bibliography   232

Introduction

Though once seen as the embodiment of religious belief in England, the Church of England and the Christian faith it proclaims is just one of many faiths both studied and practised in twenty-first-century England. As it becomes increasingly marginalised, pushed out to the edges of society, many wonder if its primary workforce, the ordained clergy, are becoming an endangered species. In order to try and understand the potential effects of this, the past thirty years have seen a burgeoning of research examining clergy life. Much of this has centred on their marital and work relationship, and on stress levels. The latest research, *Affirmation and Accountability* (2002), a report put out by the Society of Martha and Mary, looks at these and other issues.

Why did I embark on this research project? My involvement with the Church of England goes back over many years and I have been married to a clergyman for 40 years. For the last 12 of these he was an archdeacon. I have been a Bishop's Selector for 10 years and a Bishop's Visitor for nine. Consequently I have considerable experience of interviewing both those seeking ordination, and those whose marriages have broken down. As a practising psychotherapist I have spent much time over the years talking in depth with clergy.

This has enabled me to see at close hand the effect on the Church of England's front-line workforce of the various changes that have occurred over recent decades. I have heard their pain and their joy, and have also been involved at a very personal level as a vicar's wife for 28 years.

The Cracked Pot is the result of research for a doctorate carried out between 1996 and 2000 in two dioceses in an effort to gain as wide a view as possible of the way clergy live today, and to analyse the problems confronting the clergy of the Church of England. In order to provide some comparisons, a northern and a southern diocese were chosen. The research was based on incumbents who serve parishes at the 'coalface' of the Church's ministry – the visible face of the institutional Church in a parochial setting. From the 347 clergy contacted with the initial pilot study questionnaire, 76 per cent responded and 170 clergy expressed a willingness to continue the research through in-depth interviews; this number seemed unmanageable, and a random sample was therefore taken. Eventually 60 clergy were interviewed, some being unavailable for various reasons at the time.

Total sample of those wishing to continue with the research project: 170

NORTH	Single	Married	Divorced	Widowed	Remarried	Gay
Male 91	16	73	1	0	0	1
Female 9	2	5	2	0	0	0
Total 100						
SOUTH	Single	Married	Divorced	Widowed	Remarried	Gay
Male 65	8	55	1	0	1	0
Female 5	1	3	0	1	0	0
Total 70						

Figure 1

Total of random sample: 64

NORTH	Single	Married	Divorced	Widowed	Remarried	Gay
Male 33	6	25	1	0	0	1
Female 4	1	2	1	0	0	0
Total 37						
SOUTH	Single	Married	Divorced	Widowed	Remarried	Gay
Male 24	3	19	1	0	1	0
Female 3	1	1	0	1	0	0
Total 27						

Figure 2

The data collected from these interviews provide the bulk of the material within this book.

The Focus of the Research

Studying the whole body of clergy in the Church of England was not possible. Many clergy do very different types of work with varying pressures. Extra-parochial clergy usually live in their own homes, financed by a higher salary than the parochial clergy stipend, though with a mortgage. The pressures on clergy spouses in this situation are less evident, as they are not seen to be part of the ministerial post and thus have fewer expectations laid on them. They can seek their own employment without comment from a congregation and may show as much or as little interest in and support for their partner's work as they wish.

It is in the parish that the clergy family is most exposed, adding to the pressure of clerical duties. What employment a clergy spouse (still more often a wife) is engaged in, and how this affects their partner's ministry to the congregation and community, may be discussed in a very public way. The way the clergy couple bring up their children, for example how they cope with teenage rebellion, is clear for all to see and remark upon.

The use of the parsonage house, the level of hospitality and welcome, and the extent to which the partner is involved in the life of the church, seems to be part of everyone's business. For the partner, this can feel intrusive and impertinent. In particular, a wife can feel lonely and isolated, finding it hard to find her own role in the area, let alone the possibility of making friends who care about her as an individual rather than as the incumbent's wife.

For this reason, this research concentrated exclusively on parochial clergy – those who hold the bishop's licence to officiate as incumbents within their own parishes. It did not include interviewing the clergy spouses, as the research aimed to explore the incumbents' perception of their work, faith and family life. Work done by Kirk and Leary (1994) has examined data from interviews with clergy spouses.

The Context of the Research in the Two Dioceses

1. Wealth/Poverty

This enterprise highlighted certain differences between the northern and the southern diocese. In the northern diocese there is a small area with a professional population and wealthy churches. However, as the bishop said, 'In this diocese in the west there is rural poverty of a kind I've never seen before . . . in the east, urban poverty.'

A larger percentage of the northern parishes I visited were very poor, with extremely high unemployment figures. In the southern diocese I saw no real poverty. In fact, many of the parishes visited were middle-class communities. Many clergy, however, had multiple benefices, with people in the area resident only at the weekend.

This has occurred within the Church of England. Historical and sociological changes in the nation have moved it from centre-stage in society to very near the edge. In spite of this, the Church is still fodder for the media and the Press at every opportunity.

Falling Church attendances, the ordination of women priests and the misdemeanours of a few clergy are broadcast far and wide. The pressures from within, and those exerted from without, take their toll on its workforce, the ordained clergy. Nowhere is this pressure felt more keenly than by parochial clergy. This research explores the psychotherapeutic needs of those parochial clergy who were not only engaged in, but also affected by, the 'earthquake'.

Earthquakes crack structures and tear them apart. The symbol of the Christian faith, and therefore of the clergy, is the cross – a symbol of brokenness and seeming defeat. In exploring clergy needs, themes of disintegration and falling apart were woven throughout the material. Yet in spite of the cracks and fragmentation, the Church and the Christian faith aim to offer a message of Resurrection hope.

The research was a painful experience for those who took part, as well as for me. Having been a clergy wife myself for over 30 years, to see, hear and feel the pain of these 'cracks' among the clergy was profoundly moving. However, the courage of light shining through the cracks of vulnerable men and women was also seen and heard.

This work may well have been about reparation. That is not only the psychological task but also the task allotted to the Christian Church. Restoring the image, whether of a cracked pot or a fragmented person, is the aim of every psychotherapeutic endeavour. If, through the work of this research, the Church and the hierarchy are better able to see and understand the psychological needs of their clergy, and provide some specialist help and backup, the endeavour will have been worthwhile.

Conclusion

The research concluded that the hypotheses suggested at the

beginning had some basis in reality. The fact that the media and national culture are largely antagonistic to the Church establishment undoubtedly had an effect on the clergy. They felt a sense of dislocation from the rest of the nation, and wondered if their identity still had any credence within the culture they lived and worked in. Those clergy who were able to survive, and appeared to do so with success, also exhibited a greater sense of ego integration. As will be seen, this has implications for the selection of those training for ordained ministry.

Chapter 1: The cracks appear

The pressure of change

The pot he was shaping from the clay was marred in his hands.
Jeremiah 18:4a

There were just two days before the holiday season began when
the phone rang. It was the bishop. A vicar had just walked out on
his wife and moved in with a new partner. The bishop was asking
me to visit the abandoned wife on his behalf.

Such marriage breakdowns are common in society generally
and cause little stir. However for some citizens in public life,
such as politicians and royalty, these situations are useful fodder
for the avaricious needs of the media.

Over the last 20 or so years the clergy have also, to their cost,
found themselves the target of the press for a wide variety of
reasons:

'Carey urges clergy to cast dull sermons into the wilderness . . .'
(*The Times*, 23 April 1997, p. 6); 'Clergy's abused wives speak out
. . .' (*Independent*, 21 April 1997, p. 3); 'Vicar acquitted of stealing
cheques . . .' (*The Times*, 25 January 1997); 'Drink aid for vicar . . .'
(*Express*, 25 February 1997, p. 19); 'Shoplifting priest faces ban
from pulpit . . .' (*Sunday Telegraph*, 16 March 1997, p. 1); 'Bishop
insists on men only to take hospital communions . . .' (*Guardian*,
17 January 1998, p. 11); 'Bishops call for ban on ordination of
gay priests . . .' (*The Times*, 1 August 1998, p. 2); 'Gays can make
better parents says churchman . . .' (*Daily Mail*, 27 November
1997, p. 2); 'Every day another church is closed . . .' (*Independent
on Sunday*, 19 October 1997, p. 11).

This often negative public focus on the clergy's activities has
produced a sense of stress within the institutional church and
has often caused extreme trauma to the individuals through such
exposure.

To judge by the headlines in the national Press it would seem

19

that the Church of England, and the clergy who serve the Church, are experiencing a crisis within their work, their faith and their homes. Whilst acknowledging the media's tendency to sensationalise, there is nevertheless cause for concern in such communications:

Many believe that the clergy in the Church of England feel under threat of attack from all sides. The national Press writes about the clergy in anything but flattering terms. The saga of the 'Duelling deans facing new demand to quit . . .' (*Mail on Sunday*, 9 March 1997), was fodder for most of the media paparazzi during the 1990s. This is not to say that the Anglican Church does not at times deserve adverse publicity. The reason it finds itself highlighted in the press is often because of the misdemeanours of its clergy and adherents in some form or another, and the public have a reasonable expectation that the clergy will act in ways befitting their sacred, as opposed to secular, calling. In addition, the Anglican Church is still the national State Church, and the Archbishop of Canterbury is second in importance only to the Queen herself. Therefore, when the archbishop makes a comment, whether it is 'off the cuff' or a well-thought-through speech, the Press is there to report it.

So what is happening within the Church of England, and is there cause for concern? In order to put this into context, there is a need to explore various developments over the past 100 years which affected the Church of England and its place in the nation. This will help clarify why Anglican clergy feel under greater pressure than ever before.

Historical Changes

Hastings, in *A History of English Christianity 1920-1985*, traces the changes in the Anglican Church over the greatest part of the last century. His particular interest is to explore the change in status and role of the Anglican clergy. He looks at the influence the Church has had in politics up to the Second World War and the gradual eroding of that influence since then – politically, socially and spiritually. Alongside this, Hastings notes the greater professionalism of the cleric, the emphasis on a call to vocation, and the implementation, of necessity, of a rigorous theological training from the 1930s onwards.

Since the early years of this century, the state of the Church of England and its ministers of religion has changed out of all recognition. Back then, churches were comparatively full Sunday by Sunday, and the parish church and its Incumbent were accorded a central place in the community.

People often went to church, not only seeking spiritual solace or pastoral care from the clergy but because they had little else to do. The many and varied distractions to be found by the end of the last millennium and the beginning of this new one – television, Sunday shopping, car boot sales, and all kinds of leisure pursuits – did not exist. Going to church was a way to pass time in a busy if physically demanding way of life, a way to meet neighbours – in short, an opportunity to socialise. Best Sunday clothes were worn to visit a building of distinction and reverence in the community, and the Cranmerian[1] language was a source of inspiration for many. However, the clergy themselves were often seen to be ineffectual, less occupied with the needs of their parishioners than with their studies of flora and fauna or historical interests.

No longer are the majority of Anglican churches even half full on Sunday. 'The number of people attending Anglican services has fallen disastrously . . .' (*Daily Mail*, 7 February 1997, p. 16) is often broadcast in the Press, though little or no mention is made of churches where attendances are higher or increasing. The clergy could be excused for finding such headlines depressing. Recent research considers some of the reasons behind this decline in numbers.

Sociological Changes

Grace Davie, (1994), in *Religion in Britain Since 1945*, cites three areas of change in post-war Britain which have had a profound

---

1 *Book of Common Prayer,* 1662

effect on the Anglican religious life of the country. She explores the economic and social transformation in the country, demographic changes and the fact of a large influx of immigrants. These variables combined to change the religious face of the country for all time. For, as she says, 'patterns of religiosity are undoubtedly moulded . . . by what is going on around them.' (Davie, G., p. 18)

Because of the change in Britain from being a largely industrialised nation to a consumerist one, Davie believes that the resultant changes in patterns of behaviour 'colour the existence of churches and other organisations.' (Davie, G., 1994, p. 19)

Patterns of work have affected location of residence, which has seen a move out of the centre of cities into more rural areas. This has resulted in villages becoming small towns, an almost complete reversal of the Industrial Revolution, where whole rural communities moved into the towns to live and work in the nineteenth century. It was this population explosion in the towns and cities that produced the prolific church building programme by the Victorians. Now, with the move of the population out of the urban areas, the churches are left largely as empty edifices to a bygone age.

The demographic fact that 'we live in an ageing society in which the nature of family life, including the traditional codes of morality, are altering rapidly' (Davie, G., 1994, p. 3) also has affected the Anglican Church. The complexity of family life – comprising as it does single parent families, those who are unmarried, those married, divorced and remarried, those co-habiting, gay couples with children – i.e. in addition to traditional 'nuclear' families – has brought a host of searching questions to the forefront never experienced by the clergy before the war.

But it could be argued that it is the presence of a now pluralistic society which has the most profound effect on the religious life of the country. 'The arrival of significant numbers of black Christians, Muslims, Sikhs and Hindus has . . . brought a new dimension to post-war British religion' (Davie, G., 1994, p. 25). This, coupled with the influx of many Irish, Poles, and those from other European countries, has shifted religious belief away from a predominantly Anglican outlook to a multi-faith society. Thus the Anglican Church, which has been the established Church of England since the time of the Reformation,[1] has found itself challenged by the drift away from orthodox[2] Christianity. This drifting away was halted for a short time in the 1950s, during the coronation of Queen Elizabeth II in June 1953. This act 'brought together the Church of England, the monarchy and the nation in an act of sacralisation' (Davie, G., 1994, p. 31), which nevertheless had no real lasting impact. The funeral of Diana, Princess of Wales in September 1997 had a similar, albeit brief, unifying influence between the Church and the nation, as did the terrorist atrocities in the USA on 11 September 2001, when thousands poured into the churches to seek comfort and answers to their fears.

Doctrinal Changes

In recent times the archbishop has found himself under enormous pressure with regard to such vexed questions as the ordination of gay clergy in stable same-sex relationships. The *Church Times* reported 'Outrage: gay rights protesters challenged Dr Carey in the garden of Lambeth Palace on Sunday' (*Church Times*, 25 April 1997), with a picture of the archbishop and his wife looking shocked and angry. The gay issue appeared to be the sole preoccupation of the bishops in the Archbishop of Canterbury's Lambeth Conference of 1998.[3] The fact is that the Anglican Church itself has been through a period of profound change and upheaval, especially with the historic ordination of women to the priesthood in 1994. This has shaken the very foundations of the institution, which had seen little change of constitutional significance since the Reformation. The debate engendered was thought by many to be one that would tear the Church apart – and some fear it may

---

1 Sixteenth Century   2 A trinitarian faith

3 A meeting of Anglican bishops throughout the world held every ten years in Canterbury

still. That this has not yet happened has been due to compromise by the whole establishment.

But it is more than just internal disagreements about the ordination of women to the priesthood that has affected the Church. Arguments within the established Church, among the leaders, about foundational issues of doctrine – such as the Virgin Birth, the Deity of Christ, and the bodily resurrection of Jesus – have brought division to the Church, and confusion and lack of confidence to many parochial clergy. Often these clergy, whatever their churchmanship, feel angry and unsupported by some bishops and theologians, who seem to undermine the basic beliefs of the faith they preach faithfully every week.

Domestic Changes

Added to this is the growing debate on the rights of the individual; there is much to alarm the ordinary clergy. For these debates are now looking at conditions of service and whether in this day and age anyone has the right to a job for life. The possibility of the loss of the clergy freehold, once much reviled in such books as Anthony Trollope's *Barchester Towers* (1857), has brought dismay to clergy households. No longer will every ordained person be assured of finding not only a job but a house as well. Now there is more emphasis on accountability and managerial structures, as seen in the Turnbull Report (1997)[1] – principles already entrenched in business and commerce. These ideas are becoming more influential in the Anglican Church.

Living in a multi-racial, multi-religious society – where the Christian faith is one of many faiths – it seems that the clergy can no longer rely on or enjoy the dignity and respect afforded them earlier in the twentieth century, except in some rural areas. Churches are often seen as historic monuments to be preserved for posterity rather than places of worship for this present generation.

---

1 Authorised by General Synod in response to the need to streamline the Church of England

Congregations are demanding more of their clergy, higher performance rates in terms of new members added to the congregation, and a responsible attitude to resources. In part because of loss of revenue by the Church Commissioners at the end of the twentieth century, churches are having to harness and utilise the resources they have more carefully and wisely. This means a cutback in stipendiary ordained clergy, following the Sheffield Report (1974)[1]. The market economy is affecting Church life – and as a result the clergy too.

The debate on equal opportunities has affected the Church not just in the admission of women to the ordination of the priesthood. The Lesbian and Gay Christian Movement is, at this moment, fighting it strongly in the corridors of power and at General Synod.[2] They believe biblically, as well as socially, that gay Christians have as much right as heterosexual Christians to be ordained priests. This once seemingly straightforward debate, which could easily be answered by quoting St Paul (Romans 1:27), now has the appearance of a colossus as argument and counter-arguments rage. Those who adhere to a Pauline doctrinal base believe that genital homosexual acts are a perversion of God's will. They believe that God only blesses the sexual relationships of a heterosexual married couple. All their arguments they take from the Bible. For those within the Lesbian and Gay Christian Movement the biblical evidence speaks of a God of love who accepts all, whatever their sexual orientation, in loving committed relationships. It is extremely hard for two such opposing views to reach a consensus.

From this alone it will be seen that Anglican clergy are under extreme pressure.

---

1 Authorised by General Synod to investigate parochial requirements and the deployment of clergy
2 The governing body of the Church of England

Personal Understanding of the Changes

Another result of these storms is an increase in depression and mental instability amongst clergy and their spouses, and a loss of confidence in themselves, the Gospel and the Church. This was one of the primary motivational forces for such a research project. The other motivation for this research is that I myself have been part of the established Church for over 40 years, having married one of its clergy in the early 1960s. The following discourse adds my own understanding of the changing face of Anglican ministry in the light of personal experience.

During the 1960s the preoccupation amongst Anglican parochial clergy seemed largely to do with churchmanship. The focus of the clergy appeared to be on where their theological and doctrinal roots derived from. At that time there were broadly three strands to Anglicanism:

1. The Anglo-Catholic group, whose belief derived from tradition passed down through the Roman Church and then adopted into the Church of England at the time of the Reformation, and Holy Scriptures. Added to this, the worship of Mary, an ontological view of priesthood and the supremacy of the Pope as the successor to St Peter the Apostle, remained important.

2. The Liberal view of theology developed, especially during the nineteenth century, out of the liberal German theologians who were grappling with doctrine from a scientific understanding during the Enlightenment period. Liberals were seen by Anglo-Catholics and the rest of the Church of England to believe nothing and to be sceptical about everything. From a Liberal perspective there was a need to bring to bear an open mind which inquired into every doctrine with an academic rigour not used before. For the Liberal clergy there were more questions unanswered than certainties to be relied on.

3. The third major group was the Evangelical wing of the Anglican Church. In England at that time it was a comparatively small group of dedicated men who held that the Bible was the word of God and contained all that was necessary for doctrine and

instruction in daily living. The Evangelical often felt marginalised and squeezed between the powerful Anglo-Catholic and vociferous Liberal groups. Because they were in the minority, leaders within the Evangelical wing set up support groups, called Eclectics,[1] whose sole aim was to give the clergy confidence in the message they had to proclaim, and expertise on how to achieve that.

Thirty years on the scene is very different. The Evangelical group has grown beyond what would once have been thought possible. They no longer form ghettos, and many occupy roles of leadership and influence in the Church nationally and internationally. As a consequence of the ordination of women since 1994, approved by General Synod, the Anglo-Catholic grouping has decreased markedly, with several adherents moving to the Roman Catholic Church. The Anglo-Catholics who remain have been left feeling rather confused as they try to reconcile their own view of doctrine with the decisions of the Church of England's Synodical Government. By contrast, the Liberal element, though smaller, is still influential, as many liberal clergy hold posts within diocesan structures, in teaching and lecturing, and enjoy a wider area of influence.

For each of these groups doctrine continues to be of major importance in the life of the clergy, as they struggle to interpret what they understand to be the revealed word of God so that it is seen as relevant to the person in the street.

The Psychological Effect of the Changes on Clergy

However important the doctrinal debates and the fluctuations in the churchmanship lobbies continue to be, there has arisen another phenomenon that is of particular importance. This is the psychological effect that being clergy in this generation has on

---

1 Started in 1955 by Prebendary John Stott when Rector of All Souls, Langham Place, London

them, irrespective of the theological position to which they adhere. For, whatever the doctrinal basis of belief, clergy have to live in the real world, amongst real people, and in real situations. Although their belief system is vitally important, how the clergy live that out within their families, congregations and community is also of great interest, as is the effect of the wider 'world' on them.

In almost every congregation those in the pew will often accord their Incumbent considerable respect, and will accept teaching as though from God himself. This puts the clergy in a very powerful position. However, this power produces its own stress. To whom do the clergy go with their fears, their doubts? How safe is it to show human vulnerability?

The nature of parochial work, which is seen to be about proclamation of the Gospel, as well as pastoring and caring for all within the parish boundaries, inevitably creates stress. Clergy are like mice on a wheel – going round and round in circles. They are always trying to be God's representative, especially to the needy and yet, from time to time, feeling within themselves a deep sense of not being good enough or ever achieving enough.

In studying the needs of clergy, issues to be addressed are what makes a person wish to be at this interface – representing God's power on one hand, and being aware of personal frailty on the other – and become an ordained Christian minister? How much is that to do with an individual's faith, and how much the result of a particular upbringing? These are questions that need answering.

The problem of suffering, which can be used as an intellectual discussion topic amongst theological students, takes on a different hue when face to face with a life-threatening disease, a fatal accident, or an 'Act of God'. At this point, the well-worn evangelical line that 'original sin' is responsible for human misery cuts little ice when talking with grieving parents at the bedside of their dying child.

The way to become a Christian, especially for the Evangelical, is through Jesus Christ alone. Where there is uncertainty and doubt, how can the clergy keep their evangelical zeal? Or do they, in these circumstances, let go of their first theological intensity and rigidity rather than lose their faith altogether?

Evangelicals with a pastor's heart would stress God's love rather than his judgement and condemnation. However, those who find conflict and uncertainty difficult would seek a more rigid espousal of the tenets of evangelical faith as set out in the Bible. They would be more concerned about how a Christian should live, rather than look at any frailty, weakness, self-doubt and need of their own.

This latter group of clergy put all their energy into a preaching and teaching ministry. The former group, however, often see the main bulk of their work as encompassing a pastoral counselling concern, and thus being involved 'at the deep end' of a parishioner's pain and distress.

What causes this difference in approach and practical application? When both start from a similar doctrinal base, is there a tendency towards rigidity for one and an open acceptance of others for the other?

Clergy also struggle with the nature of the priesthood and its meaning within the context of parish ministry. The notion of the priest as Christ's representative carries with it very powerful images of being different from the laity. A more collaborative approach to priesthood and the notion of the 'priesthood of all believers' (1 Peter 2:9), can appear threatening to the status of the ordained priest.

Questions of how to cope with inevitable failure behind the image of the priest are seen in other areas as well. The paradox of having power and yet experiencing one's own vulnerability is not just a problem for the clergy. Feelings of never being good enough as a priest also have echoes resounding in the life of their spouse and family. Just as the disease within affects not just the work of parish clergy but their own personal spiritual journey, so the inner traumas affect every aspect of the life of the clergy.

Once the clergy were highly respected leaders in the communities which they served. This was especially true during the Victorian era, though already they were beginning to be caricatured by writers who felt they occupied sinecures. Today this is not the case. Clergy are no longer seen as having a 'divine right' to anyone's respect, and only earn that by being who they are, rather than through ordination into a role. Historical and social changes have moved the Church of England from the centre of the stage, for the most part, to the periphery of national life. This has had an incalculable psychological impact on clergy, and on their identity and sense of self. Coupled with this are the theological debates which have blown through the Church, leaving many clergy feeling disorientated and insecure. These 'cracks' experienced by clergy open more widely as a result of disagreements with basic tenets of the Christian faith as expressed either by members of the Church's hierarchy or prominent theologians. Even so, many clergy testify to the increasing need in a disjointed and disillusioned society for the sacraments of grace, which they minister as servants of the Living God. Though this in itself offers great hope that the ordained ministry will continue to be needed, it also contributes much of the increasing pressure experienced by clergy. It leaves them feeling that they can 'never give enough' in terms of pastoral care to assuage the voracious needs of their parishioners.

This research looks on the one hand at how all these changes have affected clergy in their sense of identity; and on the other at their sense of being needed as never previously by a world that is beginning to recognise that materialism and consumerism are unable to address the deepest human needs and longings. It highlights the effect of the present social and economic climate, not just on clergy themselves, but also on their families. At the time of writing this is being exacerbated by the Church of England having to make large-scale financial cuts, which will impact both on the family budget and clergy job security. The 'cracks' mentioned above are revealed by the interviews in showing the vulnerable position clergy still occupy in their communities, pulled between a role of spiritual leadership and a secular society. But as will be seen, these 'cracks' may either be fissures of destruction, or openings of blessing and grace. Ordained ministry is a sacrificial calling to use their personal inner fragility in the service of God. The following chapters explore how the clergy interviewed coped with the demands made on them, and whether they felt the Church as an institution provided the support they needed.

Chapter 2: The holy calling

Why they were ordained

> *Then I heard the voice of the Lord saying,*
> *'Whom shall I send? And who will go for us?'*
> *And I said, 'Here am I, send me.'*
> *He said, 'Go and tell this people . . .'*
> Isaiah 6:8-9

Why do some Christians want to be ordained? Why would they risk all to be incorporated into what appears to many to be little more than another club? For those who do, the words of Isaiah echo a challenge from Almighty God Himself, to leave all, to care for the poor and vulnerable, and to preach the Gospel of salvation.

This is movingly expressed in contemporary language in Dan Schutte's hymn 'I, the Lord of sea and sky', which reiterates the words of Isaiah's response of offering oneself in obedience to God's call to care for his people. It is a call that cannot eventually be denied, as many a clergy spouse can testify to their own cost.

As one of the national Bishop's Selectors, I am constantly made aware of the seemingly 'good and lucrative' positions people are prepared to sacrifice, and their willingness to embrace the attendant changes, both financially and in living arrangements for spouse and children, in order to fulfil what they believe 'God is calling them to'. For many it is a complete change of direction – from a business, commercial, educational or scientific, but essentially secular environment, to a religious modus operandi.

In spite of the clarity of this call to ministry, which is often affirmed by Incumbents, friends and family, it is no easy matter for prospective clergy even to reach a Church selection conference. The candidate must secure the approval of the Parochial Church Council[1] (PCC) before any thought of attending a conference is voiced.

---

1 The church governing body within each parish.

The Diocesan Director of Ordinands[1] (DDO), may then take a year or more to explore their vocation with them. The DDO may send the candidate to be questioned by experienced clergy or pastoral counsellors to see if they are spiritually and emotionally suitable to attend a Selection Conference. The DDO will also meet the candidate's spouse several times and ensure they are supportive of what is being planned. On average, it takes two years before a candidate reaches a Conference to test their vocation. The Conference lasts for 48 hours and is a very rigorous examination of the candidate under eight criteria (Appendix 2).

With so many obstacles to navigate, why do candidates persist in seeking to achieve their goal of ordained ministry?

In order to try and answer this question, I looked at the back-grounds from which the clergy came. How much did childhood experiences influence their adult decisions in their career or life choices?

Pie chart to show the reason for ordination of the clergy interviewed

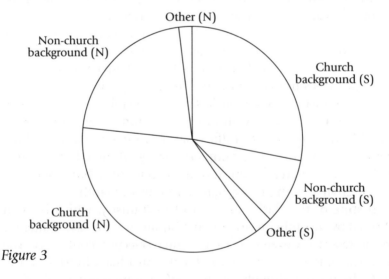

Figure 3

---

1 Every diocese has at least one DDO, whose role is to explore candidates' vocations

The above chart is interesting. It shows that by far the largest percentage of all those interviewed from both north and south came from Church backgrounds.

For many that meant they were 'born into a Church environment' because their parents went to church, their father was a minister, or, even if parents were not churchgoers themselves, they sent the children to Sunday School. In one way or another, they experienced in some depth as children a religious environment which was extremely influential in their adult formation, especially their religious espousal. It was the importance of the influence of coming from a Church background, or not, that dictated the main categories explored under the heading of 'Why they were ordained'.

Much of what follows uses the words of those interviewed.

Reasons Given for Being Ordained from:

1. A Church Background

(a) A Familiar Environment

Many of the respondents coming from a Church background described themselves as 'having grown up in it'. Attending church regularly was part of the rhythm of their life. For many it was embedded in their whole family life. For others at boarding school, daily attendance at chapel, as well as on Sunday, was part of the culture of their educational environment. Families were also often involved in community public service. One clergyman said, 'My parents were local councillors and mother was Chairperson of the Rural District Council.' For those who were either sent to Sunday School, or attended with friends without encouragement from parents, it became an integral part of their lives.

(b) A Safe Option

One participant, a married woman in her late 40s with no children, explained that she had gone into the Church as she did not want to 'enter the world of work, didn't want a career'. This woman had grown up in a vicarage, and had known no other life than one dominated by the Church. She said, 'I was happy to do nothing', and felt it was 'a way of avoiding real life'. The wider world seemed strange and alien, and she had had little real contact with the world outside her home.

She needed to feel 'safe', so entering the Church work structure, first as a 'lady worker', provided a haven. A 'lady worker', or accredited lay worker, was the only authorised employment option in the Church of England for women at that time. Though her experience of home life had not been easy because of her mother's volatile temperament, which led her 'to get things out of all proportion', the known appeared nonetheless more manageable than the world outside.

(c) A Refuge

There were, however, others for whom going to church became seeking a refuge, an identity, a place to belong. A priest described himself as a lonely boy whose parents had split up when he was a child, when he was sent to boarding school. He described becoming ordained as 'God setting the solitary in families'. Throughout his interview he mentioned influential men whom he had met and talked with. He talked about a need for his 'scars to be healed' and about the importance of such people as Archbishop Ramsey, whose books he had read. Freud's assertion is relevant, that for such a person 'religion is nothing more than a dependence on the sovereign father' (Meissner, 1948, p. 58). It was this deep sense of loss, from which powerful emotions were released, that was rooted in his search for wholeness. This is not to suggest, however, that all the respondents who came from a Church background were ordained in order to heal their internal pain.

(d) A New Family

It is interesting to note that for several respondents who did not grow up in church-going families and yet were sent to Sunday School, it was the 'family atmosphere' of the Church that attracted them.

One priest went as a young boy to a very 'lively church', but as an adult he tried to 'get away from the call and become a jet pilot'. He said that he came from a background where it was thought that those who wanted to be ordained were 'one step away from being mentally certified', according to his parents. His parents thought he 'was barmy', as they wanted him to do something 'nice and respectable'. In order to please them he went and worked in a bank for a year but could not get away from the 'inner conviction' that God wanted him to be ordained. For this person, his basic needs were not met through the ethos of his family.

(e) Upward Class Mobility

Thirty years ago, when this same priest was ordained, 'the Church' was still a respectable profession. No longer is that the case. To what extent was being ordained then equated with being 'upwardly mobile' in a class classification? Clergy lived in much larger houses than the majority of people. They enjoyed the respect of the local community, and in some places still do. In addition to this they have a clear public role.

(f) Separation from Parental Bonds

One vicar was brought up in a Christian home and though he felt 'called' to be ordained, he had a strong desire to engage with his faith on his own. This was especially true as his father was ordained, and an evangelical clergyman. This priest moved from a fundamentalist approach to faith, to a sacramental expression of Christianity, where being a priest had a greater sense of being set apart by God for holy things. He felt he sought ordination because of his need for 'affirmation': 'I was an unhappy child, always competing with my siblings for my parents' affection and time.' His father was a busy hospital chaplain and his mother worked full time.

(g) Maternal Deprivation

It could be argued that this same person experienced limited 'holding' from a mother busy with the demands of his other siblings

35

and work outside the home. Certainly, during interview, he appeared nervous and very fidgety.

He was young and vulnerable and, after my interview, I wrote down that I felt 'the Church was the loving, accepting family and father' that he had not experienced as a child. His maternal deprivation was being addressed in an institution that is often described as 'Mother Church'. That particular expression is used by Anglo-Catholic clergy who see the calling to ordination as to an ontological state setting them apart from others. From this, not only is the sense of inadequacy treated but there is also a patriarchal structure in which to begin to develop the 'I am'.

This 30-year-old had the insight to realise that in part his calling to the ordained priesthood was to address these issues. Like many other respondents he admitted that it was impossible to have his desires fulfilled.

(h) Like Father, Like Son

One priest grew up in a clergy family and felt he had wanted to be a vicar like his father, 'ever since I could remember.' At university he became disenchanted with the Church and religion, though still feeling he wanted to be ordained. After university, he went to a Selection Conference and was not recommended for training. He said he was 'devastated and very cross', especially as he was told not to return until he could 'show industry and achievement'. His Director of Ordinands said he would not be able to be 'captain of football' without playing the game.

It was interesting to note that this man had what he described as an 'idyllic childhood until 13 years'. He had good communication with his father. They then moved, and his father suffered a breakdown, and thereafter was no longer emotionally available to him. How much was his need for reparation part of his desire to be ordained, though he neither went to church nor was interested in Christianity? Of his going to boarding school he said: 'It was the first time I'd been to church without Dad being there.'

Emerging Themes

In listening to the stories of the journey taken to ordination, certain similar themes echo in the silence again and again: the need to belong, a desire for safe enough holding, for affirmation, acceptance and a wish to be the 'first-born, eldest child' – meaning that, until comparatively recently, an incumbent was the king in the particular kingdom of his parish.

Even though there is much emphasis on collaborative ministry, and candidates are selected for their ability to work alongside colleagues, there is still a view that the Incumbent is in ultimate charge in a parish. Congregations promote this idea, and older clergy come from a culture where the priest was set firmly on his pedestal. This seemingly inviolate position is strengthened by the 'uniform' that is worn (or mask that is adopted), and by 'working for God'. Because of this clergy are afforded a special place within the Christian community, right at the heart of the 'family' of God.

Discussion

There is no denying that the majority of those interviewed for this research had an experience of God 'calling' them to this work. The lack of respect for the Christian Gospel, as highlighted in the first hypothesis (see p. 14), seemed not to be a deterrent to their desire for ordination. Many felt they would be able to make a substantial difference to society's view of Christianity. In exploring further, deeper psychological reasons for wishing to be ordained emerged.

A female priest said, 'The call began when I was a child. I knew I had to work for God.' She did not come from a Church family, though she was sent from an early age to Sunday School and so had a background rooted in the Church. She said that she was always 'cushioned by love of family and friends'. She describes how things changed for her at puberty, when sexuality 'hit' her. In the past especially, religion has ignored the importance that such innate human drives and needs have for a person.

Freud has enabled the Church, or rather forced the Church, to be cognisant of human drives and desires. The woman now ordained priest will need space and time to explore being a sexual female in what was once a society led solely by men. However, her need to feel accepted and affirmed sexually will require her first to own her femininity and not to displace it all on Mother Church, as has been done in the past. The issues of gender within the Church has been a hidden subject since the time of Augustine of Hippo in the fourth century, though worked out in terms of power and hierarchy.

I was surprised by the lack of a feminist theological forcefulness within the female clergy I encountered. Either it had never been there, or other battles they had been engaged in had been so 'bloody' that they had no 'fight' left in them for this particular struggle. Many had previously been lady workers. A lady worker's role was seen solely as ministering to the women and children in the parish. Accredited lay workers usually had no liturgical or preaching role in the church, received very poor remuneration and had little or no social kudos.

For those who have grown up within a Christian family, or been familiar with life within the Church, ordination provides, initially, a return to the familiar. It accepts the person, provides affirmation of who they are and because of its institutional and hierarchical structures, provides a 'good enough parent'.

It is no longer seen to be true, as Freud originally postulated, that all religion expresses a pathological need. However, neither can such a need be dismissed. The women in the sample portrayed a seeming lack of aggression and yet they had been the ones who had stayed within the Church of England while acrimonious debates occurred as to whether they should be allowed to be ordained priest. They had also experienced, since ordination, clergy from the traditionalist Anglo-Catholic and Evangelical Reformed wings leaving the Church of England because of them.

During the one-and-a-half-hour interviews this was barely mentioned by the women, though the men opposed to the ordination of women were very vociferous concerning their own feelings. It appeared that what was most important for the women was that now they were ordained priests. They belonged in the family, occupied what many of them felt to be their rightful place and were accepted and affirmed. Now all their energies were consumed with getting on with the job rather than analysing their feelings about their new roles.

In the in-depth interviews with the women clergy, seemingly less complex psychological reasons for ordination were expressed. Maybe it was because the right questions were not asked, but the feeling was that it had more to do with the women now 'resting' where they were, and not wanting to explore too deeply what it meant to them. It was not because these questions were not being raised, but because time and space are needed before they can really be acknowledged and analysed.

The male clergy were more prepared to make sense of who they are and what they are about.

Many of the male clergy stated that it was a priest – a chaplain at home or school – showing a special interest in them, who had a profound influence on their future direction. This contrasts sharply with the female clergy, who did not mention any one person as a particular influence on them in childhood.

There was little evidence to support the idea that those who have grown up in Christian families or gone to church from a young age are more secure within. For many the desire to be ordained had an element of 'returning to the womb', reappropriating something familiar and known. For those whose fathers were clergy, there was a desire to please and seek approval from a father imago. One priest said, 'My parents were thrilled I was going to be ordained, for the Church was seen to be professional, respectable and decent.' He described the Church as a 'benign family'; again, a place of acceptance, where he felt affirmed and that he belonged.

Were the needs the same for those in the sample who were not from Christian backgrounds of any sort and who came into the Church in different ways? How much easier was it for them to join the Church from totally non-religious backgrounds, or was it more about rebelling against authority figures?

Reasons Given for Being Ordained from:

2. Non-Church and Other Backgrounds

Some of the clergy came from a background where there had been no church influence. Their families were uninterested in Christianity. The category 'other' denotes those clergy who, 'out of the blue', experienced God's call to ordination from an apparently infertile religious environment, though they may well have experienced the Christian faith at school. These two categories were included together, because there was very little difference between the views of the families of origin to religion.

(a) To Serve

One priest came from a non-Christian background, though he had attended a Cathedral school. He described himself as a 'non-Cathedral person' and said that the religion of the school had had little or no impact on him. However, he spent three years in the Army in the Libyan Desert. He described it as 'an evocative, spiritual place'. He came from a very affluent background, but it was in the desert, surrounded by poverty, that he 'felt one day oppressed at heart'. He took a long walk in the evening and 'suddenly the Lord made this move'. After this he said he 'felt quite different', that he had been given a commission to 'serve humanity'. He said he did not hear a loud voice but that 'it was an imperative voice that came from without'. As a result of this experience he spoke to the Regimental Chaplain, who advised him to 'be glad; to say "yes"; realise it will work out and go to church more often'. Once in England he engaged in voluntary work and eventually decided he should go to a Selection Conference to test out his vocation.

Whereas those from a churchgoing background were often looking for holding, this man appeared to show all the signs of guilt that one coming from an affluent lifestyle experiences when faced with extreme forms of poverty and deprivation. Winnicott linked 'a sense of guilt . . . to destructiveness, and on the other hand to constructive activity' (Winnicott, 1986, p. 81). What he seems to be saying in brief is that guilt is a necessary part of human growth and development – a desire to serve humanity and God.

For this man it was as though who he was, where he came from, the ground of his being, was suspect, so that for the very first time he questioned his own identity and found it wanting.

(b) To Find a Meaning to Life

For another priest it was not guilt so much as an answer to the existential meaningless of his mother's death when he was a young man. He began to ask questions about the meaning of life and to find himself 'drawn intellectually to the Christian faith'. He said that the 'idea of ordination insinuated itself' into his mind and just 'wouldn't go away'. To him it seemed a strange and alien idea to be part of the Church of England but because these thoughts would not go away and entered his everyday life, he went forward to a Selection Conference and was recommended for training.

The sense of nothingness pushed him to find an answer which had not been there before. For this man, the trigger calling to God was his experience of being wrenched away through death from the maternal object. It is in the 'experiences of the mother as a loving and caring presence . . . that the child finds a symbiotic union . . . that can serve as the basis for . . . trust, acceptance and security' (Meissner, 1984, p. 138). His mother's death robbed him of security, acceptance and trust. Turning to 'Mother Church' may have provided maternal and paternal 'arms' for him to feel held by.

(c) Faced with Mortality

The variation in conscious motive for ordination was impressive. A single woman started to go to church when she was training as a nurse because, for the first time, she was faced with suffering and death and could not answer her patients' questions. The metaphor of God the Rescuer, the Saviour, was enacted in her life when she found herself 'stuck on rocks in the sea and had to be air-rescued'. Not only was she nursing those who were facing death but, in this dramatic event, she had to face the possibility

41

of her own death and the existential terror that this produced. It was while waiting to be rescued that she 'made a pact with God', that if she came off the rocks alive and no one was injured, then she would 'explore the possibility of full-time ministry'. She kept her bargain with God, even though this stirred up the wrath of her parents, who would not speak to her for six months. Her relationship with her mother, which had never been good, never recovered.

'The thesis that religion and the impulse to belief are born out of the fear of death' (Meissner, 1984, p. 70), would appear to gain credence from her experience. Certainly there is a deep human need for restitution and salvation as compensation for the ultimate loss in death. That this woman was faced with it, not just at work but in a particularly personal way, caused her to examine the meaning of life.

Death, however, has an additional meaning beyond being the ultimate end of every human being. Death denotes all the fear of loss throughout life – the fear of rejection, and all the daily experiences of disillusionment, disappointment and deprivation which are part of the experience of human failure.

(d) Experiences of Loss

One priest also echoed themes of death and restitution. Not only had his father died when he was 2 years old but, as a result of his mother's remarriage, he was sent away to boarding school and did not see his mother for two years.

He was educated at seven schools and described himself at that time 'as living life at one stage removed.' He did not engage with anyone at any depth. He describes how, at the age of 18 years whilst in hospital with a suspected melanoma, he began to experience life in a real way. He encountered a young man who had had both legs amputated, having fallen off a pylon.

Like the female priest, he was confronted with the possible death of another, as well as his own mortality and the possibility of dying. He said, 'In the midst of all this I saw, unbidden at the end of the bed, the presence of Jesus Christ.' As he lay in bed he had been thinking that either 'God was the most important thing in life or it was a total con'. From what he described as a 'vision', he knew: 'The rest of my life would be dedicated to his service and that I would be travelling and involved with missionary work.'

Of all the men and women I met, this man was exceptionally gifted and had served abroad and in England. Though still comparatively young, he had contracted multiple sclerosis. When I met him he had just been retired from full-time ordained ministry and was again experiencing, in full measure, the paradox of serving a God who saves within a visibly dying body.

(e) A New Way of Life

All the respondents in this category experienced conflict with their families of origin, and were seen by them to have rebelled against the family culture. All described their parents as atheists, non-churchgoers, non-Christians, very anti-church, embarrassed by church involvement, having nothing to do with church. It is interesting to note that none of these men and women had experienced the Church in terms of finding a family, and a safe place to go to from the conflicts of home as children, for none of them had contact with church life whilst still at home. Some had had an initial experience of Christianity through school, whether at boarding or day school, but they were not involved in formal Christianity, unlike those from a Christian background.

What drew them out of the safety of the known into this 'mystical unknowingness'? It seemed to connect less with a sense of emotional impoverishment that those from a Church background seemed to exhibit. Even though those from Christian backgrounds spoke of a shared faith, it seemed that only by staying within the safety of the known could they experience integration. Yet for those from a non-church background, they were leaving all that was familiar without any guarantees that the new world would not prove just as false as the old one.

Speaking theologically, all expressed a sense that God had called them to know him and to share what they knew. Expressed in psychological terms, it may appear to diminish the sense of wonder and awe that these respondents experienced in their 'various encounters with God'. However, it can be seen that whether or not they were expressing their experience in spiritual language, there is 'no need . . . to insist that man's instincts are completely derived from the injury of loss; . . . religious belief . . . can represent a constructive aspect of ego functioning' (Meissner, 1984, p. 71).

For some, the reason behind their entering the ordained ministry may have been a sense of guilt, meaninglessness or death, but for others it was more to do with their experiences of existential isolation.

(f) In Order to Find a Sense of Connectedness

I arrived late at one clergyman's home. He said he admired the Greek Orthodox Church and had enjoyed, when visiting Greece, having his hand kissed by those who supposed he was an Orthodox priest too. This cleric was vicar of a small northern artisan parish. He spoke of books he had read and was reading, but it was quite difficult to get him to speak of his childhood. He was an only child, and described himself as a lonely child.

I began to take on board the significance of my earlier mistake in arriving late. He found it hard to articulate the feelings that mattered. He had been hurt by the Church of England in the past. Now it appeared I too was bent on 'hurting' him by turning up late.

During the interview I became aware of how difficult it was for him to minister in an artisan parish like his. It seemed, at times, difficult for him to engage on an emotional level. He prefaced most answers with a quotation. So why had he wished to be interviewed?

Thinking about it later, it seemed that throughout his life he had experienced a profound sense of isolation. As a child he won a place to the Grammar School, where he was ridiculed for speaking in a different way. Not only did his parents' work mean they were constantly on the move, but also his pronunciation and intellectual ability were foreign to all those amongst whom he lived. One reason for his desire to take part in this research was a wish to communicate his feelings of hurt to the Church. At the end of his contract in his previous post, his job was immediately filled. He had applied for many jobs before eventually finding a living. In spite of this there was a sense that in some unconscious way, by being ordained, he was trying to find a 'major buttress against the terror of existential isolation.' (Yalom, 1980, p. 363)

For this priest, ordination provided that buffer. With its clear structures of hierarchy, its theological intellectualism and the apparently transcendent expression of faith through word, sacrament and music, he could feel 'held' in the Church in what he described as 'aesthetic emotional feelings for Christian worship'. When it 'clicked intellectually' for him, he found the 'Christian view of the world very attractive and it aroused a faith response'. Here was someone exhibiting a real sense of impoverishment and an emotional need to experience connectedness with other human beings.

Several of the clergy who only started attending church at university, or as adolescents at school, did so for relational reasons – though not with such obvious desperation as this.

(g) The Call of God

One interviewee came from a loving and very supportive family. He appeared to be a secure, intelligent man who was openhearted and wanted 'to share God's love with everyone'. Thinking of recent research carried out by Mary Burton, (1997) where she argues that clergy enter a caring profession because of early experiences of loss and deprivation, it is rather a shock to meet someone who appears fully integrated.

He had started going to church at the age of 18 years because his friends invited him. Then he fell in love with a Christian girl. There seemed to be no awareness of inner need or emptiness. There was certainly no background of Christianity and when he first felt the call to ordination, he told God, 'Get on yer bike!' He said, 'I felt I was going mad' and it was the last thing he wanted to do and he 'hadn't a clue what it was all about'. However, the sense of being called persisted over a six-month period, and eventually he went to a monastery to work at 'A' Levels, ending up staying for ten years.

Emerging Themes

The themes that emerged from among those seeking ordination from non-church backgrounds were about profound existential issues: life and death; meaninglessness; isolation; loss. Unlike those from a church background, who needed to stay within the safety of the known, those from non-church backgrounds were looking outside the familiar for meaning. They appeared to need something that would provide answers to life. This was exemplified in the interview with one of the male clergy. However much the Church had hurt him, it had still provided him with a meaning to life, a place of attachment. He seemed to have totally divorced himself from the life of his childhood and espoused the Church as his 'family' and 'home'.

Discussion

The pie chart (Figure 3), at the beginning of the chapter high-lighted the small percentage of clergy from the south who came from non-church backgrounds. The percentage in the north was proportionally larger. Even so, the majority of clergy sought ordination from a life experience embedded within the Christian Church. Those from non-church backgrounds often experienced parental opposition as they made cultural paradigm shifts. In spite of that, many of the clergy indicated that parents and siblings now attended church. All the clergy spoken to from this category expressed feelings of satisfaction and fulfilment at the direction their lives had taken. Within the Church family they had found a reason for being. The deep existential questions that had accosted several of them were answered within a framework of belief that God had a purpose and plan for everyone's life. The fears of isolation and alienation evaporated within a familial structure that at least outwardly provided interaction with other human beings. At a deeper level the mystery of the Godhead and the 'Christian world view' for one person gave a strong sense of attachment.

All the clergy in this category had moved from the familiar to the unfamiliar. They had, however, found deep psychological meaning to their lives. It can be postulated that being ordained, in itself, addressed their psychological needs to feel safe and secure.

Conclusion

Reviewing the different stories told and themes emerging, there were, in many instances, obvious deep psychological needs being met by ordination to the priesthood, such as the fact of belonging to a tangible 'family' for those who had been sent away to boarding school or who had experienced the loss of a parent in early life. Within the Church both ordination itself, and the 'uniform', give the new clergy an immediate sense of identity and acceptance. Because they still work so often in situations where there is no other priest, affirmation by the congregation of their importance is offered swiftly – the sick want their priest to visit them, and the priest alone is seen as qualified to offer words of consolation to the bereaved.

These needs were highlighted in themes coming both from those who did not have, and those who had a background in Church life. There were also a few clergy who appeared to have no 'need' to belong, to be ordained, but were somehow 'accosted' and invited to think, maybe for the first time, transcendentally.

It was interesting to explore, as the other categories were analysed, whether clergy with recognisable psychological needs were able to cope with the vicissitudes of ordained ministry more competently than those who entered the ministry from a seemingly stable background. What would their needs be? Would those from a position of existential isolation, meaninglessness and death find all their fears answered in their religion? Would they, in fact, be able to minister more effectively because of where they had come from?

This begs the question, what is success? And how can it be quantified? This was a qualitative research project, the limitation of which is that the thesis can only research the clergy's own perception of their inner and outer worlds.

At this stage in the research it was impossible to validate any of the hypotheses. This was because the effect of the surrounding culture, and even the emotional integration of the respondents to it, only became a dynamic force in their lives once they were ordained.

This chapter, looking at why people were ordained, was the stepping stone for an exploration of their psychological needs in the life they now lived.

Chapter 3: I did it my way

Attitudes to authority

Every institution has its lines of authority. Accountability and managerial structures have found their way into the Church of England, though there is still a perceived culture that the priest is in sole charge in his own parish. Like the singer Frank Sinatra, some clergy would prefer to 'do it my way'. Clergy who are instituted into the freehold of a benefice as Incumbents swear canonical obedience to the diocesan Bishop. 'They can only be removed from their living through immorality, heresy or pastoral breakdown' (Leeder, 1997). However, it takes a long time to put this system into operation.

Over the last ten years lay people have found a stronger voice, and in some places are now more prepared to challenge their incumbents. However, there are still many parishes where that does not occur. Who then, do the clergy see as having authority over them? Several clergy, when asked that question, said they felt they were accountable to themselves.

A more important question is whether the clergy's own understanding of who they are accountable to has anything to say about their psychological health. Diocesan bishops have oversight over their clergy, and are seen as the chief pastor, or Father in God in the diocese. Because of the greater national, and in some cases international, roles many bishops assume, they are less available to their clergy now than in the past. Do clergy see their bishops as authority figures, and what type of authority figure do they look for?

For some clergy the bishop is like an absent father – never accessible when needed. Others said, 'It is nice to know they are there, but I'm glad they don't bother me, as I like to get on with things without someone breathing down my neck.'

View of Authority

Many adults appear to act as though parental figures still dominate their lives. It is as though they have acquired an internalised harsh, judgemental parent so that they constantly seem to question their own decisions and ideas. Parents who offer only conditional love and threaten punishments, which the child experiences as love which has been withdrawn, become part of the child's inner world. This often prevents the adult acquiring an inner sense of autonomy and thus from reaching a degree of responsibility. The Church of England, with its threefold ministry of bishops, priests and deacons, is seen by many to exemplify hierarchical structure. That it consisted until 1994 solely of male hierarchical figures had made it seem quite archaic.

In researching the clergy's understanding of authority, the data examines whether the Church of England's hierarchy is seen as primitive and judgemental, or benign and supportive. It explores whether some clergy have a dependent need for strong authority figures to take away the fear of individual responsibility. Those with a stronger ego and more integrated sense of self may desire greater distance from their bishops and archdeacons and show a maverick response to canonical[1] obedience.

Some clergy are aware that they owe canonical obedience to their 'Lord spiritual' (i.e. their bishop), but see no need to seek constant reassurance and approval – they appear to have had a good enough experience of parental nurture. For others, stress 'is self-imparted through a desire to prove or live up to expectations' (Marc Europe, *Monograph 38*, Ministry of World Vision).

Because clergy posts often rely on the bishop's recommendation, and many come within the episcopal patronage,[2] there is pressure on clergy to be seen in a favourable light by the hierarchy. Hence by the time one of them suffers a marriage breakdown or stress-induced health problems, there is often no way back. Clergy have an almost pathological fear of negative messages reaching the

1 The Canons, or laws that regulate Church practice
2 In which the bishop appoints clergy to the benefices in his patronage

bishop's staff lest it has an adverse effect on a possible move or 'preferment' to a more senior post. In one of the dioceses used in the research, much cynicism was expressed about confidentiality among the hierarchy, and fear was verbalised about 'anything getting out' which might prevent clergy from making a desired move to another parish or post.

So whom do the clergy regard as their final authority? The bishop? God? their congregation? Or are they the masters of their own destiny? Do those with a fragile internal structure need a stronger, more overt and visible authority to give them much needed security?

To whom or what are you answerable?

South
North

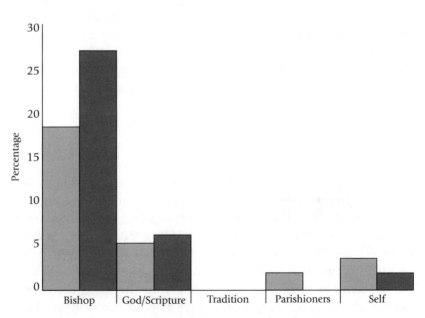

Figure 4 – Clergy Perception of the Source of Authority

These categories arose out of the data collected. No one appeared constrained solely by tradition. That may well be because the authority of the bishop, who may be seen as embodying the Apostolic Succession, is part of tradition. The Reformation did not break that particular episcopal link with the early Church. Looking at the different categories, it could be assumed that the way the clergy viewed the lines of authority denoted their churchmanship. Those from the more Catholic wing would have an exalted understanding of the bishop's power over them under God, whereas Evangelical or Charismatic clergy would see ultimate authority lying with God's word in Scripture.

From the above chart it appears that many more Anglo-Catholic clergy were interviewed than Evangelicals. This may be explained in part by the fact that the northern diocese had a higher proportion of Anglo-Catholic clergy within it's boundary at the time of the interviews, whereas the southern diocese tended to attract those of a Central churchmanship to its parishes. Churchmanship was not categorised when taking a random sample from the whole.

However, it is not who the clergy see as having authority over them that was important for this study, but rather the psychological significance that authority exercised in their lives. The data was analysed to see if the authority adhered to was in fact an 'internal parent' and if this was the case, why and what effect this had on their daily lives.

The Bishop

The majority of clergy accepted that they were answerable to the bishop. When ordained priest, the bishop exhorts the clergy to work with him as 'fellow-priests, as servants and shepherd among the people to whom he/she is sent' (ASB, 1980, p. 356). Several of the clergy interviewed felt they had been left on their own, and would have preferred the bishop to be more visible. Each of the subsequent categories were taken from the ideas the clergy expressed about the perceptions they had of the bishop, their authority figure.

1. Absent Father

One male priest felt he had 'no one to answer to on a daily basis', which he found difficult. This correlated directly with the fact that his parents divorced when he was 7 years old, and the Church became an alternative family grouping for him which was safe and secure. During his boyhood a curate took a lot of interest in him, becoming in many ways a replacement father. Now, as an incumbent, he still needed to feel there was someone there for him. He said that he had a major internal crisis when he felt he had 'misread the parish situation and there was no one to talk to'. He spoke a lot of needing someone to tell him if he was 'doing it right, or wrong'.

This particular incumbent was young and in his first incumbency. He identified a 'great gulf between being a curate and being a vicar'. For him as a curate, he still had a parental figure to fill the gap left by his absent father. He described his feelings as being like 'a blind person walking along without a stick'. For him the bishop represented his father in God, and was far more tangible an icon than the image of God. It was difficult for him that the 'bishop's authority was distant and he only told you when to move parishes'.

2. Father Figure

The image of father in God, or pastor to the clergy, describes graphically the psychological expectations the clergy have of their diocesan bishop. However, the authoritarian prerogative is derived from the fact that the bishop, in instituting a priest to a benefice, entrusts 'to a minister . . . the care of the souls within it' (Leeder, 1997, p. 73). The incumbent then has a delegated responsibility. The bishop has 'the general supervision of the clergy in his diocese and no one can perform clerical functions within the diocese without his permission' (Leeder, 1997, p. 49).

One priest felt he was 'answerable to the bishop as well as being servant of the people'. Another said that though the bishop was the authority, he was 'given a lot of freedom'. He would do something the bishop told him to do if he felt it was legitimate. It was, however, to the parishioners that he felt answerable on a day to day basis. The needs of the congregation and others imposed a 'heavy burden', as he often felt torn between 'the demands of the parish and the demands of the family'. The sense of guilt experienced by this priest and others was powerful.

Guilt is often a major preoccupation for clergy. They feel they have 'let God down', and others also, and that they can never 'get it right', or do enough. It is in this dilemma that they 'need the reassurance' that 'talking things over' with a member of the hierarchy can give.

One priest's father was a vicar. The pressure not to let him down, as well as God, the parish and the bishop, appeared to weigh heavy on him.

3. Rebelling Against 'Father'

Another vicar said that he had 'problems with authority', though he recognised that of the bishop. He spoke of himself as being a 'guilty, rebellious person' who had difficulty with diocesan figures. His father was a 'distant father'. The Church, and especially the clergy, became father figures for him in his youth. Now in his 50s, he said, 'I don't need father figures any more.' He believed he had grown to maturity and was himself now the 'father figure'. He was a rebellious teenager, and he felt he had become that again. He shared an incident when he had 'exploded' at a diocesan meeting.

The greatest problem was that not only did authority figures not have any meaning for him, but he was unsure whether he still 'ought to be in the Church of England', as he had lost his faith and 'lost touch with God'. He said, 'The traditional ways of talking about God don't mean anything to me anymore.' It was as though there was now an emptiness, a void where previously there had been a strong parent figure. He said, 'I sometimes find it hard to get motivated to work at all.' It was as though he wished to 'push away from parents both as love objects and as authority figures' (Jacobs, 1986, p. 141).

The bishop is a figure to be rebelled against, to provoke guilt within the clergy, but he is also the father who is seen never to be good enough.

4. Inadequate 'Father'

One priest blamed the bishops for not having a common mind on such things as baptism policy and homosexuality. He felt frustrated with the national Church: 'I bang my head against a brick wall.' To him the bishops were not fulfilling what he saw as their authority role. He believed 'bishops should be more hands on'. He believed they just want it 'like a sausage factory, where things are churned out'.

Another priest found the diocesan bishop extremely problematic. Because his bishop had ordained women to the priesthood, this priest had felt compelled to find alternative episcopal oversight, as he was of a 'different integrity'. He felt his bishop had let him down, first because of the ordination of women, but even more when his first marriage broke down. He said there was a complete lack of compassion and warmth which heightened his 'sense of failure'. He felt he now had a 'black mark' against his name, as he was divorced and remarried. 'Now I try to keep my nose clean and get on with the job.'

This man had had to leave his previous post due to a misdemeanour. After the interview with him I wrote down, 'He is an angry and hurting man.' At every question he needed to talk about how wrong the Church of England was for ordaining women as priests, and how much that had hurt him and others. He needed a lot of affirmation, and came into the Church of England looking for love and security. He had felt let down by those in authority for their lack of care, and by the Church as a whole. At the end of the session he said he was exhausted, but that it had 'been like a therapy session' and done him good. This sad, hurting man had been seeking, and was still looking for parental love and attention.

For those who feel so abused by the ordination of women to the priesthood, it is as though a hated sibling, and a female, has come and taken the parent away from them. One priest said 'I could foam at the mouth' because of the ordination of women, as it 'is a subversion of episcopal authority'.

5. Judgemental Father

Another priest, twice divorced, had a very great 'disillusionment with the hierarchy'. He said that 'either you become the blue-eyed boy or you are left on the fringe'. He had felt that the Church had 'labelled' him so that it was now very hard for him. He felt that he only got told off, but was never told if he had done well. In a very difficult situation he felt he was 'not allowed' to argue his case.

His father was a 'strict authoritarian' and he was totally unable to shake off the effects of his judgemental internal parent. As a boy he had 'challenged' the views of his parents, now he was challenging the Church hierarchy. For him, as for others, the bishop was not the loving father he craved.

6. Unacknowledged Father

The respondents mentioned so far have all been male. A female priest said she did not 'think about the question of authority'. Many ordained women had 'spent years as assistants . . . had discussed the value of collaborative ministry' (Dyer, 1999, p. 90). Now ordained and leading parishes, it was more important to her how she exercised that, than who was in authority over her.

Another female priest said they didn't affect her day. She got on with her work knowing that the archdeacon was there for her if she needed him.

She described her position as 'being given responsibility by the bishop and by the people to do a job'. The whole area of authority did not appear to be of primary interest to female clergy. Though one recognised the bishops' authority, she said, 'I don't take orders from them, I'm answerable to the people in the parish.' She saw the bishop as her line manager.

The concept of hierarchy, and who has authority over whom, though seen as important, appears to have less impact on female clergy than on male clergy.

Discussion

The Church of England has yet to look in depth at the psychological difference that ordaining female priests will make to the whole

Church. There was a real lack of anger and aggressiveness encountered during the interviews with female clergy. These women had grown up within a male-dominated environment. Now they were part of that establishment, they appeared less willing to challenge it. Maybe those women who are now entering the profession of the ordained clergy will be able to do so.

Though some of the clergy described themselves as rebels, none of those interviewed appeared to react adversely against the authority of their bishop or the Church. Some were quite vocal in voicing dissent from their bishop's pronouncements, but without engaging actively in anarchy. All appeared to value and need the parameters the Church sets, and also to advocate such a stance within their own parishes.

Other clergy respected the bishop's authority without question. 'The bishop should be father in God and not a line manager.' There does appear to be a direct correlation with the clergy's background in the past, and how they view the hierarchy in the present.

One priest came from a 'stable happy childhood' and said he saw the bishop as the authority figure. However, he talked more about the respect he had for those who ably and appropriately fulfil their roles. There was no sense of him feeling uncared for or neglected. As mentioned in the previous chapter, he appeared as a man with a strong sense of self.

For many clergy it was hard that their bishops were so involved in national affairs when they felt they should be fulfilling a pastoral role in the diocese. With the 'weakening of the self-confidence of the clergy (resulting) from the declining public understanding and appreciation of (their) role and no expectation of what the clergyman has to offer' (Russell, A., 1993, p. 10), affirmation from the bishop seemed even more necessary. It was not surprising that the male clergy looked to their bishops for support and pastoral care as well as acknowledging that they had the authority of the Church over them.

God/Scripture

For about 20 per cent of the clergy interviewed, authority rested not so much in the person of the diocesan bishop but in Holy Scripture. The voice of God, they felt, could more easily be heard through the pages of the Bible. The Evangelicals, especially, believed God had spoken through the prophets of the Old Testament and then supremely through the person and work of Jesus Christ. For them, God as revealed in Scripture was their final authority.

A Freudian Perspective

It is interesting to note that Freud 'had been deeply engrossed in the Bible almost as soon as he was able to read anything, and that this had an enduring effect on him' (Meissner, 1984, p. 25). Though Freud moved to an agnostic, scientific world view, the metaphors he saw within the biblical text still affected him. The Bible speaks equally powerfully to many today. Clergy who see Scripture as the authority they relate to do so because, as one priest said, in it they find 'the authority of Christ'. For him it is about 'God being in charge and wanting to do what God wants'.

Facing the Dilemma

A question that arose frequently in the context of this research was *Is God just a projection or is he, as many believe, outside, beyond? The Creator God and sustainer of life?* If he is the former, then doing an analysis of the clergy's view of God is not a problem. If, however, he is the Saviour, the Father, then how can that be analysed, or is it about analysing the clergy's perception of the God they worship? God, whoever he is, was central to each person interviewed. Because of this it was impossible to capture something that is at the core of the self and explain it, or reduce it to scientific measurement. 'God is to be found, not wholly in the world of inner fantasy, nor wholly in the world of external reality, but in the transitional world', that is, in Winnicott's terms, 'outside, inside, at the border' (Watts and Williams, 1988, p. 35).

The question to address is therefore, is it possible to investigate the transcendental? Certainly for the purpose of this survey, if

God were diminished in any way, or written out of the picture, then the heart would be taken out of what is essential to all the participants of this research.

Christian Perspectives

Christian literature starts with the premise that there is one triune God. This is expounded in the sacred writing of the Old and New Testaments of the Bible. For the evangelical Christian especially, the Bible is understood to be the revealed Word of God to his people down the ages. 'Holy Scripture containeth all things necessary to salvation' (Douglas, Hillyer, Bruce and Guthrie, 1982, p. 137).

This is a blueprint for Christian living. Though clergy who view the Bible as their final authority on all matters of doctrine and daily living will respect their bishops, yet they will only adhere to what they say if it is in agreement with Holy Writ.

The following categories arose from the interview material collected.

1. God as Supreme Authority

One vicar stated adamantly, 'God is the authority. I serve the Lord Jesus Christ and the fact I am an Anglican is part history and part coincidence.' He also said, 'The bishop hasn't got a clue what I do.' This clergyman appeared at first to be self-opinionated and full of his own sense of self. However, as he talked of his incurable illness he said, 'When following Christ we are not asked to live happily ever after.'

Through his early boarding school experience he had learned to be independent. He had given his whole life to God and, whatever was required of him, he saw it as a part of his 'pilgrim journey'. The strength of his attachment to God the Father directly correlated with the fact that his own father died when he was 2 years old. His allegiance was to the transcendental rather than a human and masculine Church hierarchy that could fail or let him down.

2. A Trustworthy God

Another priest, who described himself as a 'wheeler-dealer', said he found it hard 'to be answerable to archdeacons and bishops', as he 'didn't trust them and they were never there for support'. He felt he was answerable only to God, and found 'the worship of God the ultimate joy'. He described his childhood as happy, coming as he did from a working-class background. He was the eldest of three children. His father was a lorry driver and he said he was the 'black sheep of the family' and he 'didn't match up' to what his parents imagined 'their ideal priest should be'. His lack of trust had arisen from the time of the ordination of women to the priesthood. He was 'not against women priests, but what he was against was the liberalism within the Church of England'.

He was a traditional Catholic whose spirituality centred around the Eucharist, where he experienced God. For him, it was the God of the Eucharist, rather than the God of Scriptures that he obeyed.

Six male clergy from the southern diocese said that God was their authority. Three were modern, or central Catholics, and three were from the Evangelical wing of the Church.

3. The Incarnational God

One priest described himself as a 'rebel', saying 'lots of things happen in the parish that don't accord with the Church of England's ruling on worship'.

For this priest God was present and incarnational, in every aspect of his life. Though he respected the bishops, he believed 'God is in charge' and that he was solely answerable to him.

For all these clergy, trying 'to demonstrate the existence of God intellectually was to misunderstand the nature of God. God's way is to reveal himself' (Watts and Williams, 1988, p. 43). Each of them talked of personal encounters with God.

Interestingly, in the southern diocese only male clergy saw God as the authority they looked to. In the north, a female priest talked of 'standing in front of the King of kings' and asking 'What have I forgotten?' She did not want her congregation to see her in the place of God. She said, 'The Lord is the one to ask.' She felt she 'needed to be with God, entering into the heart of God and struggling with the pain' of ministry. She said she wished 'God would leave a note' on her pillow to tell her what to do.

Whether God is a projected father figure or is seen as 'other', the representation of God as authority will have been affected at least in part by the clergy's early development.

Discussion

The Church of England has its regulations, enshrined in Canon Law. The Christian's code of practice is enshrined in the Ten Commandments.

The whole area of authority, an emphasis on law and order, and the ongoing tension between autonomy and dependence, reflect Freudian developmental issues. All the clergy needed to have a 'figure' to relate to as their authority icon, in order to rebel against and then 'separate out' from.

One priest said, 'I sit lightly to the Church institution.' He felt it was 'broad and open', but he was adamant that God was the authority figure in his life and that he wanted to give everything to God.

This developmental stage was more easily detected in one priest, who described himself as a conservative Evangelical. His background was surrounded by church and local government. Both parents were local councillors and he described himself as being a good Anglican all his life. His father was a churchwarden. He said he came from a 'hierarchical' system. In talking about Church structures, the regularity of his prayer life in the saying of the daily offices, he came over as someone who needed to be in control. The association or link between his need for clear lines of authority, and how he coped with what he felt 'as painful rejection' will be noted when looking at the data denoting his spiritual and mental health. The fact that he said 'I can get very wrapped up with the minutiae of the system and structures' described graphically this clergyman's need for a sense of control.

Another open Evangelical priest looked to the bishop for authority, though he said that in the end he was answerable to God. It had already been seen that the *world* in which the clergy operated was seen to be out of sympathy with the ethos of the Anglican Church. This made it imperative that the clergy had security in the authority of their faith system or the institution that they were part of. This was not easy.

Each 'individual strives toward consistency within himself' (Festinger, 1959, p. 1). When a person is confronted with inconsistencies there is psychological discomfort. Festinger describes this as a 'cognitive dissonance', a state of frustration or disequilibrium which occurs when two differing ideologies or reference groups meet within one individual. Attitudes and opinions which are easily accommodated separately by the same person, cause internal disharmony when joined together. Festinger suggests that people in such a situation resort either to avoidance of the situation or to trying to resolve the dissonance.

Being prepared to integrate such differences produces a situation of conflict that is not easily tolerated.

This integration is enabled by feeling accountable to God, the bishop, or the Church. The clergyman who wanted his bishop 'to be more hands on' was alluding to the need for the cognitive dissonance to be solved through the loving care of the *father in God*. One priest talked about being accountable to God.

Several of the younger clergy from the north, during their interviews, said they wanted clearer managerial structures within the Church. One young priest said he would have valued his church having written a job description for him before he came. He felt that if he knew what was expected of him, he would have a better opportunity of being able to perform adequately.

Another priest said he found the Church's 'lines of authority' under which he worked 'very confusing'. So it was much easier for him that 'God is *the* authority'.

Clergy who looked either to their bishop or to God as their authority figure had less chance of confusion. The bishop or God represented one view of law and order, and clergy had a sense of where the arbitration was coming from. It may be that these figures 'will be heard as critical and punitive even when they are not, and even when the person has done nothing to warrant such a feeling' (Jacobs, 1986, p. 67). When bishops visited their clergy in their churches, the incumbents were anxious that everything was in order. Authority figures can cause a constant sense of guilt within.

Some clergy also experienced feelings of shame, and suffered from a feeling of not being good enough, or letting people down. Many clergy have a sense of letting God down. They are called to preach, baptise and bring people into the kingdom of God. When their churches are half empty, and they feel they and the Church are 'an irrelevance' within their community, they feel shamed and impotent in not knowing what to do.

However, as well as provoking negative feelings toward strong authority figures, the internalised parental figure may provide a positive holding. It is within the matrix of the 'family' with a strong paternal influence, whether God or the bishop, that the priest feels secure. Here the clergy can live 'at others' commands; pleasing others is high on the agenda; and seeking advice and approval is a constant factor' (Jacobs, 1986, p. 75). Dependent clergy can run 'back to daddy' when life becomes intolerable. For those who vest the authority in themselves or their parishioners, there is no such safety net.

Parishioners

When clergy spoke of parishioners, they were speaking about all the people within 'a geographical area entrusted by the bishop to the minister who has the cure or care of the souls within it' (Leeder, 1997, p. 73). The priest is responsible before God for their work amongst all parishioners, whether they are Christians, of other faiths or adhere to no particular faith group. The 'authority' of the parishioners is powerful. They will show their approval or disapproval by attending or declining to attend church. Clergy who fail to listen to the people in their parish do so at their own peril.

Some incumbents are in charge of parishes with 40,000 people, others have small country parishes with but a few hundred living there. If they have several churches to work in, the pressure on them is to cope with separate congregations and communities, who often have no desire to work with other churches in the area.

Expectations on the Clergy

Parishioners are not necessarily members of a congregation. They can (and do), demand visits from the priest and that the priest will officiate at the 'occasional offices' – weddings, funerals and baptisms – when required. Though many have little or no time for the church and its vicar, they are usually the ones who make vociferous protests if the church congregation wishes to make any alterations to the interior or exterior of the church buildings. They may never go to church yet they will have an opinion, which they may share, about the clergy, and whether they are 'caring and pastoral'. In close-knit communities parishioners will be as aware of their clergy's lifestyle, and that of his spouse and family as are the members of the congregation. Parishioners can exert an inordinate amount of influence on the life of the clergy, and the consequent stresses from these pressures are evident in this research.

This amorphous group is therefore observed to hold much power, expecting clergy to be 'on call' at all times. As a result, few of the clergy interviewed were prepared for the parishioners to hold the authority.

These categories emerged as the clergy explored their own perceptions of the power the parishioners had over them.

1. Collaborative Authority

One vicar was used to authority but did not seem to know where it was located. For him, it was in the 'churchwardens, who represent the congregation and are like colleagues'. He also saw it in the parishioners within the community, and within the hierarchy of bishop and archdeacon. Commenting on the interview afterwards, I noted that he looked and sounded depressed, and talked incessantly. This clergyman had indeed suffered from depression and was receiving counselling. For him, the interview appeared to be a chance to offload all his fears and inadequacies.

He had three churches to care for, with a total population of 5500 people. He said, 'I am very much on my own.' He also said that 'the time you spend with an authority figure is small because everyone is so busy, unless you have committed a terrible crime'.

2. Accountability

A southern female priest had a very pragmatic view of authority. 'The parishioners have authority over me,' she said, 'because they pay me.' She was therefore answerable to them. She had also said that she came into the ordained ministry as she 'didn't want to enter the world of work'. She had a small parish of 1500 adults and one church, in a rural area. She said, 'I will not let myself go.' As a child she had experienced significant levels of verbal violence from her mother so that, in every situation, she applied logic and reason. She said, 'I have a strong sense of responsibility to people.' Though she obeyed the Canon Law because it was the only way she could have the life she wanted, she felt strongly that she had to be true to herself.

There appeared to be a very firm wall of defence around this respondent. Maybe that was why she saw authority vested in her parishioners. Though on the one hand they made constant demands, on the other hand she had learned how to keep them at what felt like a manageable distance from herself. Authority figures, like parental figures, were harsh and judgemental in her experience, so now she quite literally shut her front door if she did not wish to engage with someone. As she said later in the interview: 'I will not allow myself to be bullied.'

A male priest described authority as being vested in 'the people on a day to day basis'. Though the bishop was over him, nevertheless he felt 'a duty towards the community'. He did what was right, 'bearing in mind the needs of the people'. He said that he was seen as the authority figure and that he didn't want to be like his predecessor, who told people what to do. He would rather stand back, but found it 'very hard to motivate people to take leadership roles'. In this former industrial coal-mining parish of about 3000 people, he said that the people in this mainly artisan area 'were reluctant to offer their gifts'.

There was a sense of hopelessness as this priest spoke, especially when he said, 'I hope God is in it all.' He felt that he was 'more concerned about things than God is', and he got very fed up that others didn't share his vision.

Discussion

Looking over the data from those priests who saw authority lying within the community, there is a sense of helplessness. Only one priest appeared to have a clear sense of direction. Her fear of violence had caused her to keep a tight hold on control; even though she affirmed that the parishioners exercise the power, yet she had erected firm boundaries beyond which she would not allow others to trespass. This interview was difficult because of the heavy defences she had erected and the fear of sharing any vulnerability. She appeared 'very precise and exact . . . planning out all that was said, perhaps afraid of letting something slip' (Jacobs, 1986, p. 65).

One priest, when talking about his churchwardens, said, 'They can always say they don't like this or that.' The themes in the data generated from his interview were about his not being 'good enough', or not coming up to expectation. Both of these clergy, in different ways, exhibited a sense of failure. Of his childhood this priest said, 'I was not a useful member of the school, but met people who were intellectually superior to me.' Of his home he said, 'It wasn't a frightfully leadership-type home . . . my father did have certain offices in the church . . . not hugely important ones.' How much his early life had been a battleground for control was not discussed. He was still waiting to feel affirmed and approved of.

Another priest felt answerable to the community on a day to day basis but also that 'the bishop has authority' over him. He was over 60, and due for retirement. He had served in the RAF during National Service and then became a schoolteacher. Through the interview it became clear that he felt he had not got the satisfaction out of being ordained that he had hoped for. His father was not very supportive of his being ordained as he felt he could serve people better as a teacher.

Tracing through the previous data and analysing the clergy perception of authority where the bishop, God and Scripture and parishioners have occupied that role, it highlighted the sort of early experiences they had had as children with their parents.

The last category to be looked at in the area of who has authority was the self.

Self

Winnicott (1965) talks of emotional development in the child/adult as a 'maturational process'. If during early development the child is deprived of 'maternal pre-occupation', or experiences loss, then rather than the human infant maturing and integrating the life stages, they will experience emotional deprivation. Their sense of self will be what Winnicott (1965) describes a false self.

A 'Fragmented Self'

Only three who were interviewed during the research revealed what might be described as a 'fragmented self'.

One priest experienced the break-up of his parents' marriage when he was a teenager. As an adjunct to the disintegration at home, he found solace as a young boy in his local church choir. He was a communicant member from the age of 11 years. He had read Philosophy, Politics and Economics at Oxford. Describing his call to ordination, he said, 'My ideals at that time were to build peace.' It was through the intellectual stimulus of reading theological books and conversing with friends that he was drawn to the priesthood. This priest could not talk of God calling him, nor was he able to verbalise any understanding of an emotional relationship with God.

He worked in a small rural area with five churches. He said, 'I'm not answerable to anyone.' He felt he was 'a one-man band' and wondered how much longer he could go on. He described the job as a 'heavy load'. Though he wished to build up a band of lay people to work with, there was 'no real sharing of the faith'.

He had been ill for some while, and at the interview he said how 'very disillusioned' he was. He felt 'the Church of England had lots of stunts to stem the tide and build bridges with people and to renew the life of the parishes', but he feared the tide was still going out. He said, 'I don't discern God's will and I've no idea who Jesus is.' He found the New Testament 'irrelevant', and everything to do with the Church and his role as vicar, he felt was an irrelevancy to those around. This very depressed and sick man said he 'felt very unsupported' and that he had to get on, on his own. He felt he was going through a crisis about God, and about the Church of England.

It seemed in talking to him that though he had recognised 'a need for healing within', and had in fact studied Jung avidly, as far as his faith was concerned it had remained an intellectual exercise. His emotions had not been engaged. There appeared to be a real dissociation between his intellectual activity and his emotional and spiritual existence.

There was a strong sense that he had no experience of belonging. He had been divorced and then remarried. There was a deep inner exhaustion that emanated from this priest.

There was an equal sense of dislocation when interviewing another priest. His wife had very recently left him so that he felt: 'The only authority I'm answerable to is what I impose on myself. I'm answerable to myself first and then to God.' He felt that the authority figures – archdeacons and bishop – made no impact on what he did and showed no interest in it either. 'Where are they?' He had little time for bishops and wanted 'to see them as far away as possible'. He said, 'Since my wife has left I have not heard from a bishop.' When he had first arrived at his parish four years previously, there were some very difficult issues that needed resolution. The bishops were not supportive. He said, 'I don't look for help from bishops now, as it won't come.'

Because of all that had happened to him, he said his faith had been rocked: 'I stood up in church and said, "If God is sitting there, would you mind standing up and waving so I can see who you are, because I'm not quite sure where you are."' He had lost confidence in what he was doing and felt he had lost his way with God. He was very shocked by his wife leaving as he felt he had been trying for twelve months to make the marriage work.

Though he said God was distant and he could not find him, he believed his faith would come back. He said that the good thing that had happened was that he had 'learned to depend on other people'. Before this he was closed to others. He had been the carer and the giver, but now he was learning to receive.

It is important to note that these two respondents who believed authority was within themselves were males who each had a failed first marriage and had experienced major trauma as a child.

One priest's father died when he was an infant and his mother did not marry again. All three found the boundaries of their lives first during the years of growing up, and then as adults, disintegrating. No longer were there any safe structures to hold on to. All three were well over the age of 50, and the sense of a life that had not fulfilled expectations had added to their burden of distress.

Discussion

The mid-50s are a difficult age for incumbents. If they have been in their parish for some years, they may feel they need to move before they reach 55 years old, because no other parish would want them as their incumbent. At this age they may also feel passed over by the hierarchy. As one priest said, 'I don't feel my gifts have been properly appreciated in the wider Church.' He was voicing an oft-expressed view of disaffection, that he had not been considered for preferment to a more senior post. This can leave many older clergy experiencing weariness within the job they may have been doing for many years.

In this situation the sense of aloneness often appears as a lack of integration. In different ways these three respondents all expressed this, though two of them appeared to be working through their traumas.

Conclusion

None of the women priests fell into this category. '(Their) new ministry was marked by liberation after years of waiting, a release of energy which had been suppressed . . . Many spoke of a sense of change in their inner being – of becoming who they were meant to be through ordination' (Dyer, 1990a, p. 86). Their preoccupation now was with the work they were doing and not with who they were. The women interviewed were certainly not anxious about who had authority over them. Neither were they preoccupied with a sense of guilt that they were not coming up to the 'bishop's expectations'. It was as though they still lived within the afterglow of their ordination to priesthood.

Dyer, (1999) in her paper on *Reviewing the Reception – Five Years of Women Priests*, has found women now ordained reluctant to resurrect old wounds. Dyer is involved in work amongst women who have been harassed and abused by male colleagues. She experienced frustration that so few women are prepared to reveal 'situations where they have felt themselves to have been bullied or sexually harassed' (Dyer, 1990a, p. 3). She believes they are 'reluctant to speak . . . because of their fear that they will not be believed and that the institution will protect the men concerned' (Dyer, 1990a, p. 3). This is certainly true. However there was another reason why they did not come forward.

These women had 'fought' for many years for the right to stand alongside male clergy and to preside as equals at the Eucharist. This had involved them in innumerable confrontations with authority figures within the Church. Though many bishops openly supported their petitions, many still did not. Even now, in at least three dioceses women are not ordained to the priesthood by their diocesan bishops. For those who had been ordained and were now incumbents, the battle had been won. There may still be barricades to storm but the main one has fallen. During the interviews, there was a sense of 'arms laid down'. Unlike their male colleagues, they did not have such a need for a dependent relationship on their bishops. They had now come of age, were no longer tied as 'children' to an underling's role within the Church. They could exercise authority too. Though none were yet ordained bishops, there was every expectation that this would happen. For now, the women were enjoying the freedom and autonomy that being ordained priests gave them.

This may link directly, though often unconsciously, to the sense of threat the male clergy felt, and their need to feel accepted and affirmed. During the interviews it was very apparent that the whole notion of authority was important to them – not only their own exercise of leadership within their parishes, but also to whom they were accountable. Few relished the idea of just getting on with the job. The majority of male priests wanted to know that their bishop knew what they were doing and was interested in them.

Many bemoaned the now largely national role played by bishops, which prevented them from exercising a more pastoral role within their diocese. Clergy expressed dismay when 'yet more academics or managers' were appointed to the House of Bishops, because they felt their diocese would miss out on pastoral care. They appear to need strong authority figures. In what way does the clergy's view of authority affect their understanding of what it means to be a priest? Are the two inextricably tied up together?

The next chapter will seek to answer this question.

Chapter 4: To be or not to be . . .

What it means to be a priest

The question of how the clergy saw the role of the priest, and what meaning it had for them, was the hardest section for them to address. This was not surprising. 'The Church of England is a notoriously enigmatic institution. Clergyman, Minister, Parson, Clerk in Holy Orders, Priest, and Vicar: this range of designations indicates the variety of ways in which the religious functionary of the Church of England may be regarded' (Russell, 1980, p. 3). Add to this Rector, Priest in Charge, Curate, Non-stipendiary, Worker Priest, Ordained Local Minister, and Minister in Secular Employment, and it is not surprising to find such confusion. However, the above titles given to the clergy have a historical derivation. It is not the purpose of this research to pursue a historical modus operandi, nor will it further the pursuit of the emotional needs of the clergy to investigate a wholly theological exegesis of priesthood.

Theological Understanding of Priesthood

However, to understand the clergy's view of their role and status as priest, and how this informs the whole of their life, it is important to set the research in a theological context. Russell (1980) remarks that the word 'priest' is a theological definition. This understanding is grounded in the New Testament writings, and the subsequent development over the centuries of the doctrine of ministry and priesthood.

'Clergy', and the other terms mentioned apart from that of priest, denotes an occupational role. The word 'priest' highlights the ministry as vocational and theocratic.

How marginalised many clergy feel by society has already been discussed. Because of the implications for the clergy of the irrelevance of the Church in many people's lives, it is even more crucial that their view of what and who they are produces self-confidence, rather than undermines their self-image. Understanding the meaning of the word 'priest' will also allow exploration of the clergy's psychological needs within this category.

The idea of priesthood comes initially from the Old Testament (Leviticus 8:12) when Moses anointed Aaron and his sons. Aaron was the first Levite to be ordained priest. In the New Testament Jesus Christ is seen to be our 'great high priest, who is able to sympathise with our weaknesses' (Hebrews 4:15), through his death on the cross and resurrection. All Christians are described as 'a holy priesthood, offering spiritual sacrifices acceptable to God through Jesus Christ' (1 Peter 2:5). 'There is (then) no New Testament warrant for ascribing any special qualification of priesthood to ordained persons within the common priesthood of the church' (Sinclair, Ferguson and Wright, 1988, p. 531).

It was in the third century that bishops and presbyters (elders), influenced by Cyprian, were designated as sacrificial mediatory priests. At the Reformation and through the influence of Martin Luther and others in the sixteenth century, the Church was called back to the New Testament understanding of priesthood. However, different views of priesthood continued.

The conflict centres round the enactment of the Eucharist. This 'Thanksgiving' service represents the Last Supper of Jesus Christ, where he used the broken bread and wine poured out as a picture of his own impending death on the cross for all humankind.

In the Church of England there are those who take a more Catholic position on this and therefore venerate the 'Blessed Sacrament'. But there are also those at the Evangelical end of the spectrum who view the Holy Communion solely as a service of remembrance, reminding them of all that Christ has done. Within these extremes there are many variations. The issue for this research, however, is about how the clergy view their own priesthood. Is it the sacrificial priesthood of the Old Testament, which denotes an ontological position – that is, 'once a priest, always a priest'?

The laying on of hands by the bishop is seen to change that person in some mystical way so that at the altar they are 'Jesus' for people, as the Revd Lucy Winkett said (BBC 2, 27 June 1999) in a programme about St Paul's Cathedral. Or does ordination confer eldership on the clergy? The bishop says at their ordination:

> 'A priest is called by God to work with the bishop and with his fellow-priests, as servant and shepherd among the people to whom he is sent. He is to proclaim the word of the Lord, to call his hearers to repentance, and in Christ's name to absolve, and to declare the forgiveness of sins. He is to baptise, and prepare the baptised for Confirmation. He is to preside at the celebration of the Holy Communion. He is to lead his people in prayer and worship, to intercede for them, to bless them in the name of the Lord, and to teach and encourage by word and example. He is to minister to the sick, and prepare the dying for their death. He must set the Good Shepherd always before him as the pattern of his calling, caring for the people committed to his charge, and joining with them in a common witness to the world.'
> (*Alternative Service Book*, 1980, p. 356)

This debate continues and it is interesting to note which of the extremes prevails at a particular point in Church history. That may well denote the strength or otherwise of the Anglo-Catholic, Liberal or Evangelical constituencies within the institution at that time.

In order to understand the clergy view the data was divided into five groups denoting their view of their own priesthood – Representative, Pastor, Servant, Shepherd, Teacher. Figure 5 shows the result. These categories were symbols used by the clergy to denote their own view of the role they fulfilled.

View of priesthood

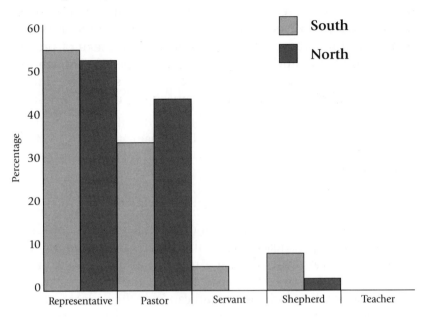

Figure 5

Producing a chart proved difficult. In rereading the transcripts, many of the clergy's answers were confused. The assumption was made that Anglo-Catholics would see themselves as having a representative ministry,[1] whilst Evangelicals would place themselves within the 'pastor' and 'teacher' columns. That assumption proved to be not wholly accurate. In reality most priests saw themselves in more than one category. The problem was resolved by studying the individual interviews and placing each priest within the category that appeared most faithfully to represent their own view of priesthood. Though this system had obvious weaknesses, the frequency with which the clergy spoke of themselves according to one model of priesthood gave the exercise enough validity to ensure its credibility.

1 Representing Christ to the people and the people to Christ

Michael Ramsey's book, *The Christian Priest Today* (1985), is at the top of the reading list for many aspiring ordinands. He offers four responses to the question 'Why the priest?' He says the priest is 'a man of theology, a man of reconciliation, a man of prayer and a man of the Eucharist' (Ramsey, 1985, p. 10). Though he sees priests in a representative role, he does not see them 'becoming Christ'. Nowhere does Ramsey say that the priest is 'Jesus for the people'.

Self-image

The work of the priest is a lonely occupation. Several of the clergy at interview were exhibiting signs of clinical depression. It appeared that with the breakdown of their defence system, they were left feeling exposed and vulnerable. Ordination to the priesthood can provide not just a role but also a mask to hide behind. A person can feel set apart through the Episcopal laying on of hands at their ordination, and can hide their inner feelings of low self-esteem behind a 'godly' exterior. Such adults often seek leadership roles in order to attempt to restore their own self-image.

Why people are ordained and how they perceive the authority structures in their lives delineates the view they have of themselves. This is most clearly seen when looking at what the role of the priest means to them.

Evangelical priests see their role in terms of a pastoral and didactic function, whereas the Anglo-Catholic priest has a pre-eminently sacramental[1] role. Evangelicals lead from the front, in the sense that they are not 'above' or 'beyond' any within the congregation. Anglo-Catholic clergy, with an ontological view of priesthood, see themselves as separate from the laity through the laying on of the bishop's hands. They are, in an incarnational[2] way, being Christ for, and to, the people. Though this varies

---

1 The priestly function at the Eucharist is at the heart of Anglo-Catholic spirituality
2 God taking on human form in the person of his Son, Jesus Christ

widely across the different expressions of faith among the churches, this broad division is generally accepted.

How much, then, does the clergy's self-image determine their view and understanding of priesthood? One respondent to the research said, 'I sometimes wonder what I am doing when I am holding up my hands at the Eucharist.'[1] He felt at times that his enactment of the Eucharist felt flat and empty. Was that due to the fact that he came from an Evangelical background with a notion of the priest as a leader and pastor? He had no sense of his role being part of the 'otherness' of God, though he had moved towards a more sacramental form of ministry.

The Anglo-Catholic, because he represents Christ, is seen to be apart from the world. The distance, and the fact that clergy are empowered to anoint the sick and absolve the sinner may enhance self-image and this may remain so even amidst criticism and conflict about their ministry because of its sacramental nature.

How much is this self-image enhanced by the notion of the priest as a sacerdotal image and how much is it diminished by the notion of being a pastor to unwilling sheep?

However priests see their role, their understanding of their self-image will have been laid down in childhood long before they heard the call to represent the Wounded Healer[2] and Suffering Servant[3].

Few people are immune to the desire for a good self-image. Though ordained ministry is about forsaking all for Christ's sake, concerns about the image they project are important to clergy. Robes still worn since the sixteenth century have no 'particular doctrinal significant (and) . . . are not to be understood as imply-ing any doctrines other than those contained in the formularies of the Church' (Leeder, 1997, p. 297). In spite of that statement, the dress – that is, a black, grey or other coloured clergy shirt and the robes or vestments[4] worn – denote a priest's churchmanship,

---

1 The Church service that commemorates the death and passion of Jesus
2 A term to describe Jesus Christ
3 Isaiah's name for the Son of God
4 Eucharistic dress for some clergy

and are important to most clergy. Anglo-Catholic priests (often from the more traditional wing), wear vestments for the Eucharist and black shirts with dog-collars. The uniform speaks of the importance of their priestly office as God's representative – they represent God to the people and the people to God as they preside at the Eucharist. Conservative Evangelical clergy wear no vestments, and may not even wear robes for the Holy Communion service. Those in between may dress in a varied combination of these according to circumstance. Though this is a generalisation, yet again it imbues clergy with a particular perception of their priest-hood, which may have much to say about their own self-image.

It is interesting to note that a modern Catholic and an open Evangelical priest have much in common. Both would hold to the centrality of a liturgy founded on Word and Sacrament, and both are more prepared to adopt the style of dress most in keeping with the church within which they serve.

Several of the clergy said that being a priest was tied up with celebrating the Eucharist. They viewed themselves as iconic. The bishop laying hands on them had, through the Holy Spirit, imbued them with the sacred and the holy. In some churches congregations venerate their clergy, calling male priests 'Father'. How much is this to do with the teachings of the Christian faith, or is it more to do with the need of some clergy to wear a mask which disguises their fragility?

Analysing the data from the interviewed clergy, as they discussed what being a priest meant to them, may help in understanding the image clergy have of themselves, and whether the 'uniform' of the priest might be a defence against a fragile interior.

Representative

'A person authorised to act or speak for others' (*The Collins Pocket Dictionary*, 1981). As can be seen from Figure 5, the largest number of clergy saw their ministry in the 'representative' category. Even amongst that group, however, there was confusion as to the definition of 'representative'. It hovered between the Catholic view of representing God to the people and the people to God, and the more Liberal view of the one who visibly represents the priesthood of all believers. What significance lies behind the meaning for the clergy? The categories emerged by inference from the clergy interviewed:

1. The Dissatisfied Leader

One priest said that a priest is 'an altar person . . . leadership is very important'. He saw himself as a leader/pastor. His father was a distant, 'absent father'. He described himself as having problems with authority. His 'whole life had been a battle to learn how to be a father', which he felt was more important than his job. However, what was extremely significant was that he felt the Church had not used his 'gifts'. He would have liked to have been 'a mover and shaker', but found himself in a job that was boring, and wanted to break out. During the interview he said, 'I would like to be a bishop or archdeacon. How do you do that? I can't apply for such jobs. Some people in the hierarchy are not my equal.'

In discussing his rebellious feelings and lack of faith in God, it seemed as though the only tangible element still left was presiding at the Eucharist. There he could wear his uniform and regain a sense of authenticity.

He expressed not just a sense of failure but also of envy. Klein, (1957) in her discussion of the concept of envy, believed its roots were in deep primitive feelings of frustration and desire. This man's desire to be a bishop or archdeacon could, in Kleinian theory, be linked with early infantile experiences.

Whilst 'God' or the bishop provided a 'parent' for him to relate to, he felt safe. When he experienced separating out and became father to his own inner child, then 'violent destructive impulses (made) their appearance' (Spillius, 1988, p. 123). Thus was engendered his eruption at the large meeting. He said, 'either I get a job like that or move out to some other job.' His representative role was not secure enough to prevent him from leaving.

2. The Intruders

It has already been remarked upon that the ordination of women to the priesthood has had a profound effect on male clergy. Female clergy, having achieved what they had so long desired, appeared more integrated in their view of themselves and their understanding of their role as priest. The men, however, for the first time, have become aware that gender is an issue that the Church must grapple with. Before 1994 it seemed possible to banish such discussion from the Church's agenda, as it was not on public view. Now female priests with a high profile are performing what has previously been a male prerogative, and this issue can no longer be ignored.

'Sexuality is as basic for the survival of our species as food is for our individual survival' (Jacobs, 1986, p. 86). Gender issues produce envy and rivalry, whether amongst siblings or within peer groups. The ordination of women to the priesthood has done just that. Male clergy have served 'Mother Church' as representatives of all that is potent and virile. Now that women have intruded, however, there is much uncertainty as to how to include them into this male world, and a real fear of men losing their power and authority.

Historically, Chapter[1] meetings have been notorious for the lack of caring fellowship and for the insidious competitiveness that is generated. These meetings are for clergy to meet and support each other, and discuss matters of mutual concern. In many deaneries clergy will avoid going because they come away feeling undermined. Female clergy often do not feel accepted in such gatherings. They find such meetings particularly difficult in the light of the veiled suspicion they receive, accompanied by the fear of some male clergy that they will usurp posts they might otherwise be in line for.

3. The Uniform

One priest said: 'Being a priest is representing the people.

---

1 A group of clergy meeting within a specified deanery area

Wearing a uniform is a sign that God is here.' He was very conscious of his weaknesses and vulnerability and said, 'I would like people to like me and to think I am friendly.' He believed that what he did at the Eucharist defined him and that his role helped him to relate to God. He was 30 years old and single and the description written about him immediately after the interview was: *He is a young, anxious man, who recognised his need to please and his fear of confrontation.* It was also noted that he appeared to have a history of mood swings and becoming depressed. He would need his 'uniform' to act as a defence against a seemingly hostile world outside.

Though his childhood seemed happy, he remembers his parents arguing, and 'hating' his sisters for long periods, and fighting with them physically. He began to show an interest in going to church at the start of adolescence and was confirmed at the age of 17 years. The Church and its uniform had provided him with a sense of identity. Being a priest, for him, had made him feel he belonged.

4. A Sacrificial Role

Another priest saw himself as an intermediary, bringing people to God and God to the people. He said, 'I have a love relationship to God which is basic to my priesthood. Self-offering is key to priesthood. You have to give yourself away time and time again.' He believed pastoral ministry is about 'self-giving and associating oneself with the cross'.

This priest was very aware of his failures, and that he could not live up to people's expectations of him being a 'holy man'. He had broken his leg some months before the interview. During his stay in hospital he realised he wasn't 'in control'. He had had to learn to be dependent on others and had found that very therapeutic. He had celebrated the Eucharist in a wheelchair and had people wheeling him around. It felt as though any defence system he had built up had been pulled down, and he was now ministering just as he was.

A young, single priest said, 'It is hard for me to look at my role as a priest.' He had come from an Evangelical background, but now had moved to a Catholic expression of his faith. He believed priesthood was 'about sacrifice' and, though he found it hard to articulate, expressed it as 'being available, loving, accepting, kind, strong, prayerful and committed'. Several times he said, 'I still have the L-plates on.'

He was on a learning curve in every area of his life, friendships, preaching, meetings and parishioners. However, he did not feel he was one of the people and said: 'I am different and have a very high profile.'

5. A Holy Work

Two of the priests believed that the 'priesthood is a particular office and calling within the Church that has to be safeguarded, as it is under threat'. They believed the priesthood was 'holy, sacred and God-given and couldn't be chucked around like confetti'. One priest said people saw him as God's representative, though he saw his ministry as about affirming 'everyone's ministry'. He believed that people were being ordained too easily in the Church. By this he meant many were being ordained as non-stipendiary clergy. For him that was not being a 'real' priest.

Another priest said: 'I am a priest in the order of Melchizedek,[1] a priest for ever. I can't step in and out of the role, as it affects every part of my life. Wherever I am, God is there as well.'

Discussion

1. The Women

If the male clergy found it hard to define priesthood, though it had been a male preserve for 2000 years, how did the female clergy cope? For them, the ordination to the priesthood did not seem to be the defining moment in their ministerial lives. As one said, 'I've been ordained three times – as a deaconess, a deacon and now as a priest. I have felt a priest of God all my life, as I had a platform from which to share my understanding of God.' She

---

1 An Old Testament priestly figure

did feel less frustrated now she was a priest. She had a sacramental view of life, 'handling the holy in people's lives, in the world God created and in sacramental mysteries'.

Another female priest said the sacrament was very important to her. She said that 'the marks have been rubbed out that were there before ordination'. She had felt she was short-changing people but now she could do what people expected of her like any 'normal' minister. For her, it was a fulfilment of all she had wanted over the years, along with the other female clergy.

One priest described herself as 'Christ's representative' but went on to say that she was 'a point of contact between God and people, a facilitator'. For her the important thing was that she now had the authority to offer a sacramental ministry.

Many of the women seem more concerned with what they could do for people than with the image they reflected. Their struggles with their self-image had been more basic. It had felt that it was *not good enough* to be a woman, for you could only be a second class citizen amongst church full-time workers if you were. Being priested had therefore confirmed that God had created women as well as men in his image (Genesis 1:26-27). For men it seemed that being a priest was about adding another dimension to who they were.

The Eucharist represents brokenness as well as wholeness. In sharing in the brokenness of Christ and of his world, the priest partakes in Christ's resurrection life. 'It is about transformation and transcendence.' For those who saw priesthood as representative, the Eucharist was central to their lives. As one priest said, 'It takes a large amount of time in my life.'

2. The Men

Francis and Rodger (1996) studied the influence of personality on clergy role prioritisation, role influences, conflict and dissatisfaction in ministry. They found that the main body of Anglican male clergy was introvert. Such people find social gatherings difficult, public occasions embarrassing, and would prefer to hide away. They did not evaluate whether there are more introverts among the modern Catholics than amongst the open Evangelicals. No doubt the Catholic view of priesthood would provide a defence behind which the introverts can hide. Though for many of these clergy pastoral work is important, the emphasis on a salvific Eucharistic ministry, seen as distinctive and separate from lay ministry, provides them with a safe distance from others. When feeling dissatisfied with the job, the representative role provides a sense of authenticity.

Each of the clergy in the column marked 'Representative', said the fact of being an ordained priest was the most important thing to them in their lives. All of them saw who they were in terms of a sacramental ministry, which was rooted in worship and the Eucharist. Though many seemed confused about what the term 'representative' meant to them, they agreed it was about having a unique, sacrificial, holy role.

Many of these clergy, male and female had found profound fulfilment in their calling. They, maybe the women especially, had found out something important about who they were. They had a real *raison d'être*. However, it was also apparent that even the clergy who had such a high view of their calling, found that priestly accoutrements were not themselves proof against the disappointments inherent in the job.

What about those who saw their role mainly in pastoral terms? Were they less likely to experience disappointment because their self-image was less ontologically rooted?

Pastor

'When all is said and done the increase of . . . love of God and neighbour remains the purpose and the hope of our preaching of the Gospel, of all our Church organisation and activity, of all our ministry' (N. R. Niebuhr, 1985, p. 1). 'Pastoral care is the practical outworking of the Church's concern for the everyday and ultimate needs of its members and the wider community' (Atkinson and Field, 1955, p. 78).

Nowhere in either of these definitions has a sacramental ministry been mentioned, yet all those who saw their priestly role in pastoral terms were engaged in a sacramental ministry. All were called to bring people to repentance and in Christ's name to absolve, baptise and prepare for confirmation. They were also exalted to lead people in prayer and worship and to preside at the celebration of Holy Communion.

Pastoral care has the notion of being alongside the vulnerable and weak – a 'hands on' outworking of a priestly function. As such, it is also about willingness to be vulnerable and open to others.

Many of the clergy who saw themselves primarily as pastors would use the word 'minister' rather than priest to denote their calling. This distinction, though theological, 'has nonetheless, important practical implications for the way that the role is carried out' (David, 1994, p. 174).

Many of these pragmatic roles that clergy have been involved in through the centuries have more recently been usurped. Once clergy were instrumental in education, medical care, welfare work and, especially, ministering to people's emotional needs. Now such works have been taken over by professionals, whether within the state or the private sector. What has been especially hard for the clergy is that it is now often psychotherapists or counsellors who have taken over 'ministering to', or working with the emotionally deprived or traumatised.

Nevertheless, if clergy make themselves available to their community they often find, especially in this market economy, that the clergy are 'the only available person to whom the most vulnerable turn when there is no apparent alternative' (Davie, 1994, p. 176). Therefore clergy became generalists though still functioning on a priestly level as well. How does this affect the self-image of the pastor clergy, and therefore what needs does it produce?

The categories highlighted were implicit in the words of the clergy and are descriptive of the work they do.

1. *Showing God in All They Do*

One clergyman believed clergy are there to act 'as a focus of prayer and study, to show God through service to the community'.

He hoped that people would see him as 'approachable and open with them' and that they could discuss anything with him. He kept reiterating how human he was and that it was very important to know himself. He was prepared to baptise anyone's child and marry divorced people, as he believed 'everyone is entitled to God's grace'. He admitted that sometimes the dog-collar could be a barrier, and because of that he was happy not always to wear it.

Another incumbent described himself as an 'Anglo-Catholic Charismatic'. He was 61 years of age and saw his role in practical pastoral terms rather than in ritualistic ones. He said, 'A priest is a link between God and the world. He is not a representative but a conduit – that is, an element of communication.' He described his role as 'standing in the front of the crucifixion and seeking the sorrow of God and his brokenheartedness and his rejection by people'.

He had been 20 or more years in his parish and believed that was important. People knew and trusted him and he saw second and third generations as well. He described his ministry as a 'glorious and wonderful vocation' and he felt a sense of fulfilment that he was doing 'something exceedingly worthwhile'. The fact that he met people right where they were, he said, satisfied his need for self-esteem.

This clergyman was brought up in an affluent lifestyle amidst great poverty. The guilt experienced and the feelings of low self-worth resulting from this appeared to have found solace through ministering and caring for others.

2. Proclaiming God's Word

Another priest said, 'Being a priest is nothing to do with presiding at the Eucharist.' He preferred the word presbyter, or elder. 'Someone recognised and reasonably experienced in things of God and pastoral work.' For him the whole emphasis of his ministry was on 'proclaiming the word of God'. Though he called himself a pastor, he found, as a single man, that it was difficult to do much pastoring. Unlike the previous priest, he felt he needed to share difficult situations with others so that he himself did not become too embroiled.

He described his home life as a very happy and very loving Christian home. His father was a London City Missioner, so that he was used to the ministry of care. This clergyman seemed quietly content, not a recluse, but certainly with a strong integrated ego. He enjoyed his own company.

Unlike those who saw themselves as having a represent-ative role, these clergy spoke little about the Eucharist. Their emphasis was on people and on their needs, rather than a mystical experience.

3. The Suffering Servant

One priest said that he 'identified strongly with the wounded healer'. He wished that people saw him as 'the servant', serving God who is 'the Servant of the world'.

Another believed he was 'wrestling with others to allow God to be real'. He saw himself as 'just part of the whole congrega-tion, trying to let God work in us'.

This priest came from an Anglo-Catholic background but said he had now come 'to have a very low view of the ordained priest-hood'. He described himself as not naturally a leader, though he knew that was part of his role. He owed a lot to the Charismatic[1] Movement, and all that it had enabled him to understand in terms of healing and God at work in power. Even so, he got frustrated because he found in reality that the vision was hard to realise, as it never quite works. 'I wrestle with the people and with God and say, "Why the hell are you not doing here what you say you will?"' He said he often felt like a small boy having tantrums.

This emotional man had experienced tragedy at first hand when his son died in an accident. For him, wrestling in prayer with God was his ministry.

The two female clergy in this category saw themselves not as sacramental priests but, as one stated, 'the wounded healer or

---

1 A movement from the 1960s which emphasised the work of the Holy Spirit.

suffering servant'. Again for them it was about coming alongside the weak and vulnerable, and ministering God's love.

All these clergy were prepared to move out to others without hiding behind a mask. They seemed aware of their own inner hurts and longings, and talked openly about them. Several of them said they had been 'touched by the Holy Spirit and had found a deep fulfilment of joy and power in the Holy Spirit'. Their longing to share that, as well as become partakers with others in their lives, provided a very different flavour to their ministry than to those whose root was centred in sacramentalism.

A 'Modern Catholic Charismatic', who was struggling through depression within an economically deprived parish, could still say 'I must identify with others' suffering, cry with them, laugh with them'. He said: 'If I can do that, then I will have achieved something.'

4. *The Care-giver*

A priest whose father was an Anglo-Catholic vicar said, 'I become less and less sure what this thing "priesthood" is, and also less clear about what the work is.' Having discarded any idea of sacramental priesthood, he seemed to have little to put in its place, though he said 'the job is to recognise the worth' of other people: 'Now I prefer to work with non-church people, especially those I encounter at funerals. I used to think the Eucharist was everything. Now I'm more drawn to what the Bible is all about.' He described his family, and parents in particular, as 'undemonstrative, with no real touching'. It appeared that now, in tentative ways, he was reaching out 'to touch others' in order to find a real sense of self.

One priest described himself as 'a guide and fellow traveller'. The emphasis again, was on 'being with' rather than 'apart from'. It was also about being 'himself' and finding his own identity in the role he assumed.

An acknowledged homosexual said, 'I lost friends when women were ordained priest.' He found he was not invited to dinner, or sent Christmas cards by members of Forward in Faith. He believed there was not one sole model of priesthood, and that he did a U-turn when women were ordained priest. He found it a great shock to realise he had been wrong about female priests, and that when they were ordained 'the roof would not fall in'.

He had enjoyed working with women clergy, and it had helped him to reflect on the nature of priesthood in a different way. Now he saw the priest 'as playing ball amongst the people, as a pilgrim leader, leading them on, snapping at their heels like a shepherd dog'. He stood with people and travelled with them. He said he had a happy childhood, though it had been solitary. He was an only child, and his father was ill with tuberculosis. Again, there was a sense in which this man was seeking to be 'in touch'.

Discussion

Several of the clergy who saw themselves as pastors shared the pains they had been through. It seemed that often these experiences had been defining moments in their lives and brought them face to face with themselves. They had faced major crises, whether divorce, depression, or a son being killed. They had to face existential isolation and meaninglessness, expressed by one when he said, 'Why the hell, God, aren't you doing what you said you'd do?' It is at such a point that God becomes for them a *life-giver*, or they lose faith in him, as another priest did. Such crises are either instrumental in a meaningful continuation with the struggle of a pastoral ministry, or produce a cynical reaction with nowhere left for clergy to go.

Servant

'I am among you as one who serves' (Luke 22:27). Jesus constantly emphasised his servanthood. He was on earth to do the will of his Father in heaven in all things. He exhorted his disciples not to be concerned about 'which of them would be the greatest' (Luke 9:46), but to be prepared to wash each other's feet. It is not surprising that 2000 years later those with a vocation to follow Christ into full-time ministry are 'called by God to work with the bishop and his/her fellow priests, as servant and shepherd among the people to whom (they) are sent' (*Alternative Service Book*, 1980, p. 356).

Two clergy only, one from the north and one from the south, saw their role of priest exclusively as that of a servant. Many of the other clergy included servant as part of the role of priest, though these two had a greater sense that priesthood is synonymous with servanthood.

The Human Servant

One described himself as a Protestant in doctrine but a Catholic in worship. However, being a priest for him was about 'suffering'. He was suffering from a progressive illness but felt called 'to teach people how to die'. He said, 'It sticks in my gullet when I hear priestly ministry described as gaining a superior avenue to God, or that priests are superior beings.' For him, priests are like anyone else – human, and therefore 'in the same boat as everyone else'. He therefore saw his role as 'being there for others'. Much of his pastoral ministry and energy had been spent seeking to provide facilities for the underprivileged.

It is interesting to note that if the index in a book on psychology or psychotherapy is explored, words like 'suffering' or 'servant' seem to have no place. Why is that? The emphasis on Freudian, Jungian and other psychologies, whether analytic, cognitive or behavioural, appears to be on 'wholeness', 'maturation', 'indi-viduation'. For the Christian, the theological centrepiece is the cross – the salvific work of redemption. In Philippians 2, Paul describes graphically the willingness of Jesus to leave the glories of heaven to become 'nothing', in order to serve and save fallen humanity. So when exploring the psychological needs of Anglican clergy, it is almost impossible to do so without using theological language.

'If anyone would come after me, he must deny himself and take up his cross and follow me' (Matthew 16:24). For many Christians, this is a clarion call which can neither be dismissed nor laid aside from the whole message of the Gospel. Jesus spoke about being among his followers 'as one who serves' (Luke 22:27). The 'servant' priests in the research sought to follow his example and to use their gifts of love and pastoral care to try and meet the needs of the lost and bewildered.

There is a general feeling that the western world has become both individualistic and self-centred. Some have laid this at the feet of psychoanalysis. Freud was, however, a realist. Just as the Bible and Christians emphasise the fallen nature of humankind, so Freud believed that 'what history tells us and what we ourselves have experienced rather justifies a judgement that belief in the 'goodness' of human nature is one of those evil illusions by which mankind expect their lives to be beautified and made easier while in reality they only cause damage' (Freud, 1961, p. 104, and Meissner, 1984, p. 161).

Nino, discussing Augustine of Hippo's search for the restoration of the self in his Confessions, says that the quest for truth is at the heart of both genuine religious experiences and the therapeutic method, and that it comes from the willingness to 'recognise oneself for what one is' (Chadwick, 1991, p. 12).

In this search for religious experience, there are certain themes which arise especially from the concept of a servant priest – sin, guilt, betrayal, doubt and wholeness. These themes are at the heart of a priest's search for a meaning to life, and an awakening understanding for a restoration of self. They are seen to be woven into both the religious and psychodynamic realms, and it is in exploring them that a person is enabled to recognise themselves for who they are.

Discussion

It is these very themes which highlight for the 'pastor servant' the heart of clergy work. As one priest said, 'Being a priest is dangerous to health and feelings of comfort. You cannot expect to be fulfilled. The work is mostly enormously frustrating.' He went on to say that if he engaged with the community then he had to give himself and it was 'an ongoing sacrifice in time, well-being, material things, and in effort'. It was for him about having to 'join with Christ on the cross', where themes of sin, guilt, betrayal, doubt and wholeness meet (see Appendix 3).

Maybe one of the reasons that only two of the clergy saw themselves primarily in the servant role is that it is such a costly role in spiritual, physical, emotional and mental terms. It is about identification on a psychological and spiritual level. Rather than hiding behind a mask, it is as though all the inner and outer defences are down.

Shepherd

Three of the clergy interviewees saw their priesthood in terms of being a shepherd. Again, this was a direct reference to Jesus, who said, 'I am the good shepherd' (John 10:11). The shepherd of Old and New Testament times, and still in Israel today, went in front of the sheep and led them. Though many Christians have an antipathy to being called 'sheep', the idea of the priest as shepherd is deeply symbolic for many clergy.

1. The Leader

The priest as a representative has a mystical quality; the pastor is the priest who goes and paddles in the mud with the parishioners; the servant priest is open to personal woundedness, as well as to the wounds of others; whereas the shepherd priest is the leader from the front. Though one priest was 'not in favour of a paternalistic ministry', yet he saw his function in terms of 'leading the sheep to pasture, feeding the sheep through preaching and pastoral care'. He was 'the conductor of the orchestra trying to get each member to play to the best of their ability and to play in tune'. He said that a lot depended on him as leader and on his 'personality'. Because of this, he tried to do too much himself and forgot to delegate responsibility.

Another priest talked about the importance of leading from the front, though he saw that the 'negative side of the priesthood was having to be a one-man-band'. This clergyman talked about using lay leadership, though he said, 'shepherds lead from the front, so there is a strong element of leadership'.

2. Model of Christ the Good Shepherd[1]

One priest ministered in a small rural parish. He found its small-ness very pressurising: 'If I am needed, I must make an immediate response, as I have no excuses.' For him, the model of ministry that meant most was Christ the Good Shepherd. Though he would say that presiding at the Eucharist was top of his agenda, he nevertheless saw his priesthood as also being worked out 'in the context of the community of people'.

Discussion

Within all models of priesthood there is a strong flavour of leader-ship.

Only the younger clergy felt that they needed more help as administrators, though none of them saw that as part of the priest's role. While some saw their work in terms of evangelism, it was not mentioned under this category as an essential part of their work. Evangelical clergy, however, had a burden for evangelism, which they articulated. Leading public worship, preaching and pastoral care appeared to be their main preoccupations.

It has been noted how the representative priest had a mystical leadership, the pastoral clergy a coming-alongside leadership and the servant priest an identification with the cross – a leadership which equated with the themes of sin, guilt, doubt, betrayal and wholeness.

The shepherd leader appeared to form the end of the continuum. It was almost as though the salvific priest started with a transcen-dental ministry which was earthed by the pastor and servant priest. The shepherd priest then led the people out to the 'Promised Land'. It had a heroic feel to it – almost like a Pied Piper or Peter Pan figure, dancing ahead to the Promised Land. The Shepherd, like Peter Pan, has an untouched, unearthly quality. Both are ageless, and provide the possibility of escape from intolerable, unwanted situations.

'The prototype of a shepherd is not based on an abstraction of

---

1 As seen in the Gospel of John, Chapter 10

the characteristics that actual shepherds have in common, but on a more intuitive concept of the paradigmatic shepherd' (Watts and Williams, 1988, p. 135). Though there is much that is similar to the prototypical shepherd, nevertheless the 'Good Shepherd', Jesus, was seen as the 'ideal shepherd'. The clergy who use the 'good' shepherd as a model for ministry were then aiming to emulate the 'ideal' shepherd.

This leading to a Promised Land, 'a new heaven and a new earth' (Revelation, 21:1), Freud saw as an illusion. He felt that like dreams, they stood in the way of reality, and that one of his roles in life was to destroy illusion, for 'to tolerate life remains, after all, the first duty of all living beings' (Meissner, 1984, p. 162).

However, over the years, Freud's antipathy has been refocused so that 'the current perspective not only has found a place for illusion but has defined it as a powerful and necessary force in human psychic development and in the continuing nourishment and health of the human spirit as well' (Meissner, 1984, p. 164).

All the categories of priestly role so far studied relate directly to the clergy's sense of meaning, purpose and their destiny. The Christian faith appears to speak to the deep needs of the adherents. The shepherd priests with the 'ideal' shepherd always set before them, embody many aspects of life. Their role is one of symbolic meaning, leading their 'flock' out to new pastures, caring for the sheep and rescuing those that are lost.

There are many other symbols of faith which become important throughout life. As well as the bread and wine, the crucifix, the cross and the liturgy, the ordained clergy themselves are used by Anglicans in this way, for they are visual representations that provide a psychological mechanism for an adherence to an unseen deity. These symbols engage people on a sensory, visual and auditory level so that 'the individual believer prays to a God who is represented by the highly personalised object in his inner, private belief system' (Meissner, 1984, p. 182).

The shepherd priest becomes not only the transitional object but leads people to the 'ideal' object, with all the promise of psychic wholeness offered in such an encounter. The strain of such expectations became apparent, however, when one priest said, 'A lot depends on me and on my personality; I find I try to do too much and so need to withdraw into the desert at times.' Another priest said, 'I make too many burdens for myself and bite off more than I can chew.' The clergy were aware of the pressure of such a role but seemed unable to surmount it.

Conclusion

Looking at the research as a whole, it seems that the question of what it means to be a priest is pivotal. It is the clergy's understanding of their own priesthood which defines their role, gives them their identity and affects their relationships within the home, congregation and wider community. Their view of who they are in God's eye and in the eyes of their people will influence profoundly their spiritual and mental health. This is in line with the hypotheses.

Where clergy from one churchmanship struggle in a church with a very different churchmanship, they often feel unaffirmed and rejected. If they see themselves as representatives of God in a congregation that has little liturgical appreciation and wants a preaching Vicar, the internal struggle will affect them at a psychic level.

Because of the increasing proportion of Evangelical clergy over recent years, many of them struggle in churches that are of Anglo-Catholic or Central churchmanship. Congregation and priest find themselves at variance and both feel confused by this cognitive dissonance. This does not sit easily with them, because clergy and people belong to the same Church of England and yet speak a different language.

The Church of England seems not to have addressed the diversity of theological opinion. It has gloried in its breadth as a Church, and with justification. However, this may have been largely at the expense of a baffled laity and an already struggling clergy – for, as has already been noted, self-image is crucial to a sense of well-being. It may also be at the expense of family and friends. The clergy's understanding of themselves as priests will have a direct effect on family life, which will be explored in the next chapter.

Chapter 5: Knowing me, knowing you

Home life, family and friends

'Research concerned with the psychology of Christian ministry would be incomplete without taking into account the home and family life of the minister' (Francis and Jones, 1996, p. 321). It is also true that exploring the psychological needs of clergy must include their families and other intimate relationships. Many clergy spouses describe living in a parsonage house as being in a goldfish bowl. If the house is near to the church they feel especially exposed and vulnerable.

Married Clergy

Before discussing single clergy, this chapter will look at what makes clergy marriages different. In their book *Holy Matrimony* (1994), Kirk and Leary recognise the public nature of the clergy marriage. Like royalty, politicians and others, their home and workplace are one and the same. This is true also of farmers and most self-employed workers, and the increasing number of people who work from home with the aid of modern technology.

It is therefore important to look at what makes clergy marriages distinct from others. One bishop, when asked that, replied: 'There are differences from other marriages, and also similarities. It is the total package that makes clergy marriage a special case.' He went on to list the factors which he considered distinguish clergy marriage from others:

- Tied housing and often fixed-term appointments
- In many places a lower income in comparison to the rest of the parish
- Biblical standards of personal morality
- Living in a goldfish bowl
- High expectations from others of clergy family life
- Ill-defined boundaries between work and home life

- Doing the Lord's work – spouses may feel they 'compete' with God
- Fear of using counselling agencies when difficulties occur.

Several books have been written by clergy wives (Meyrich 1988, Nash 1990 and others), exploring the particular dimension of being 'married to the ministry'. Each of them describes how it feels to live in such an exposed situation – the intrusiveness of being so open to people's gaze; comments on how they live as a family; constant encroachments into family life of their spouse's work due to the telephone or doorbell ringing. Living in a house that is not their own produces the stress of others' interest in how the garden and house is looked after. Though there are benefits in not being responsible for the structural upkeep of the tied house, the friction and stress involved when the house needs repair often outweighs any positives. Added to this, working for an employer, 'God', whose demands appear to disadvantage the rest of the family; it is no surprise that many clergy spouses are discontented.

Ashdown (1998) writes of her experience of living through a clergy marriage breakdown and surviving the divorce. Though not as high as the national average, the number of marriage breakdowns amongst the clergy across the dioceses each year has raised anxiety within the House of Bishops.

For over ten years Broken Rites, an organisation campaigning for the rights of clergy wives who have been abandoned, have seen Bishops take very seriously the plight of deserted wives. As a result of the concern expressed, an informal working party was set up in 1994-1996, chaired by the then Bishop of Winchester. In their summary of suggestions they looked at: the stress within clergy marriages; the need to prepare couples for when the spouse is ordained; the need to offer support, and have in place a code of practice for the management of a marriage breakdown situation. However, it is still experienced by many that bishops are more concerned with keeping scandal out of the press than in addressing the increasing pressures on clergy marriages that may eventually lead to their breakdown.

There is also another dimension to this. Increasingly, clergy wives pursue a career. They are consequently neither prepared nor willing to forfeit promotion or to give up the work they are doing in order to leave the area and move to another parish. Some clergy wives are themselves ordained priests, and it is increasingly common for a male priest to give up his parish and follow his wife, whether in secular employment or work within the Church. The increasing affirmation by male clergy of their wives' gifts and expertise is welcomed by many but it also means that for some husbands it is very difficult to find employment, especially within the Church. Consequently, male priests are now experiencing the dislocation inherent in following their partners.

Distribution of married and unmarried clergy for the whole sample (size 237)

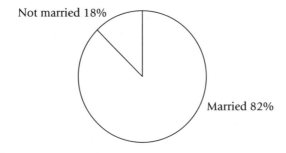

Figure 6

Initially, it was not known who had been divorced, remarried or was gay. As the research project progressed this became clearer, though even in the eventual random sample it was unclear how many of the clergy had remarried. One priest had declared himself gay. It was not, however, until the semi-structured interviews that it became clear who were describing themselves as homosexuals and in a gay relationship.

Figure 2 (in the Introduction) gives a breakdown of the various relationships before the interviews.

The eventual total number of clergy interviewed was 60. This was because one priest from the north was admitted to hospital the week he was due to be interviewed. Two others had retired, and one had moved without communicating this information.

The breakdown of numbers that were to be interviewed into the various relational categories

NORTH	Married	Divorced	Separated	Remarried	Widowed	Single	Gay
Male 31	16	1	1	5	0	4	4
Female 4	2	0	0	0	1	1	0
Total 35							

SOUTH	Married	Divorced	Separated	Remarried	Widowed	Single	Gay
Male 24	18	1	1	2	0	1	1
Female 4	1	0	0	0	1	2	0
Total 28							

Figure 7

Single Clergy

As will be seen, several male priests were prepared to admit in the interview that they were homosexual and in a sexual relationship. Nine per cent of all male clergy interviewed were gay, including clergy who said their sexuality was a grey area. This was a similar percentage to those priests who were single but heterosexual. None of the female clergy admitted to being lesbian.

The gay clergy in relationships, though living on their own, had the constant companionship and support of their partners. They did not experience the loneliness and isolation of the heterosexual single clergy. Sixteen per cent of the sample were single, of whom some were young clergy living on their own for the first time.

Of the two male clergy whose wives had very recently left them, one was on his own, though he saw his children frequently. The other priest looked after his children, who had frequent contact with their mother. Both divorced clergy also had access to their children. One widowed female priest had children to look after; the other had no offspring but had a very close friend across the road. Ten per cent of the sample had experienced separation, divorce or remarriage. One single heterosexual priest had a close female friend with whom he spent all his free time.

What effect did these relationships have on the clergy? What effect did it have on their psychological needs and how much was determined by their early experiences? In what ways did their view of their priesthood affect their intimate relationships?

Personal Relationships

Bowlby (1946-1972) worked as a full-time consultant psychiatrist at the Tavistock Clinic. It was here that he began to explore the result on a young child of being separated from its mother. Through his research he propounded his theory of attachment.

Attachment:

Bowlby described an 'attachment figure' as 'the mother figure . . . to whom a child directs his attachment behaviour by preference' (Bowlby, 1973, p. 42). He found that children who had been parted from their attachment figures to be hospitalised, suffered traumatic dislocation. The resulting body of knowledge strongly suggested that children deprived of their attachment figures would, as adults, show signs of dysfunction. They would be seeking to repair the primary damage by locating an attachment figure to provide reparation. This unconscious longing may be directed towards any person or institution, such as the Church, who seems to offer emotional nourishment.

It has already been noted that many of the clergy from the sample were sent to boarding school from a young age, or had little contact with one or both parents as a child.

100

The concern of bishops and researchers about the breakdown of clergy marriage has also already been noted. This research looked at the clergy's perception of their own marriages and support systems amongst family and friends. Some of the data related to clergy in a homosexual partnership, but all the research explored the nature of the relationship and the role it fulfilled in the life of the priest.

How did clergy view the role of their spouse? How important were spouses to the feeling of wellbeing? Even more important, what role did the spouse or the partner have in the perceived success of the clergy in ministry?

'It was evident from the research sample that many of the clergy had had difficult families of origin' (Kirk and Leary, 1994, p. 94). Not only would such clergy look to the Church as a new family and a safe environment in which to work, they would also look towards their spouse to provide that necessary figure on which to attach all their longings for acceptance and affirmation.

My research explored and compared the sense of security within those clergy who felt supported and affirmed by their spouse, and the sense of dislocation and alienation of those clergy whose marriages had broken down, or whose spouse was uninterested in their work. Interestingly, Kirk and Leary, in their research amongst Anglican clergy and wives, found that many of the clergy had 'dominant, controlling mothers and/or distant, cold and absentee fathers' (Kirk and Leary, 1994, p. 94), so that the Church becomes the benign attachment figure that will value the offering of her 'sons and daughters'. Often what is being sought from the Church is the same as what is being looked for in a spouse. Marriage and the Church offer stability and a sense of belonging.

For the single priest, the need and availability of close friendships was examined. For many, the loneliness of living alone in a community where so many expectations were laid upon them, meant that their emotional, sexual and intellectual needs were often sublimated in the work.

Because the research enquiry had been so wide ranging, it was only possible to investigate backgrounds superficially. Indeed, the aim of the first theory question was to explore why the clergy sought to be ordained, rather than attempt an in-depth study of their childhood. Even so, patterns of early emotional deprivation were noted.

In order to gain some understanding of how the clergy viewed their own relationships and what impact those relationships had on them, the following categories in Figure 8 were highlighted from the data. Many of the clergy described their partners as supportive. The other categories were implicit in all the clergy shared about their relationships with those close to them.

Personal Relationships

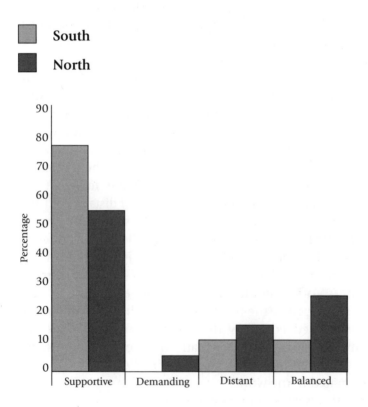

Figure 8

Supportive – Male Clergy Marriages

Kirk and Leary (1994) maintain that Anglican clergy marriages are based on companionship rather than sexual attraction. In their research they found that 'shared values and belief, similarity of background, personality, niceness, decency and stability' (Kirk and Leary, 1994, p. 55), were of greater importance. Throughout this research it is the clergy's need to feel supported that has been highlighted, whether by the parish or the hierarchy.

In interviewing the clergy about their marital relationships, their emphasis was mainly on how supportive or not their spouse was. Such phrases as 'she is better than a curate', 'she is always there for me', and 'I don't know how I'd manage without her', show the depth of dependency male clergy, in particular, had on their spouses. It was as though their wives made up for the deficiencies that they felt they had.

The importance of this report is seen in Figure 8 where nearly 80 per cent of the clergy in the south and 55 per cent in the north reported that their spouses were very supportive.

1. The Stable Marriage

One clergyman said he had 'a very happy stable marriage'. He described his wife as a 'committed Christian' who shared in his sense of vocation. His wife knew him after he had already felt called to the ordained ministry, so that it was always part of the marriage scenario. She had her own career. Her career was seen as 'every bit as important' as his. It helped financially that his wife earned more than ever he would as a parish priest. He said, 'I don't know how other clergy survive on just the stipend.' Though he was sometimes torn between the 'demands of the parish and the demands of the family', he felt his wife was there to 'support and encourage' him. Interestingly, this priest came from a non-church background where his parents had no understanding of his desire to be ordained.

Another priest said that his wife had always been very supportive and was a partner in ministry. He said his wife teaches part-time, so again there were fewer financial problems. Because he had grown up poor, he said he had a very low expectation of financial remuneration, though it had been difficult for them to manage before his wife returned to work. They try to take days off together, but if something 'important comes up in the parish' he would deal with it.

He said, 'The children learned Sundays weren't good days because I was often tired and irritable.' He concluded by saying, 'Without my wife's support the edifice would crumble.' Their previous parish had been a very tough one, and they felt they 'lived in a goldfish bowl'. His wife had become angry at the effect the ministry had on him at times. 'That has increased over the years.'

One priest described his wife as a deeply Christian woman. 'We have a close relationship to each other and are deeply committed to each other.' His wife's father was a clergyman and she had vowed she 'would never marry a priest'. Nor did she – her husband was a scientist before he was ordained!

They were both Australian, and the husband said, 'Our biggest rebellion was leaving Australia.' He had been brought up in a church environment and had been 'a model lad'. Though his wife maintains a radical independence from him and his ministry she is, nevertheless, 'wonderfully generous and supportive. She is committed to my sacrificial ministry.'

Money presented no problems for them as his wife was in well-paid secular employment. He described her as 'highly qualified and very professional'. She had been the main breadwinner, and was sought after by many people to share her expertise. However, he resented the fact that he was unable to be more financially supportive of the family. They had a disabled child. He said that 'the children have been deeply affected' by his life and ministry in their attitudes and lives. They all suffer from self-esteem problems. This was due to anti-church feelings in their schools and because their father was the vicar.

This priest said it was also difficult to maintain friendships as he had moved parishes several times. He said, 'Who wants to know you if you're a priest? I am set apart by my lifestyle and the pressures. I feel like a person with two heads.'

2. Second Marriage

One priest had been divorced and was now remarried. Though his wife had children from her previous marriage, he had none. He described his first marriage as a mistake from the start. Because his first wife had had problems as a child, she wouldn't have children. He said, 'There is a great stigma attached to divorce. I stuck the marriage for seven years because I was a priest. It then all became impossible and I couldn't carry on even if I lost my job.' In reality he did not lose his job.

He said, 'It's quite difficult for my second wife being married to a priest, as she can no longer be an ordinary person in the congregation. Though there are no expectations on her, it is what she can't do that is difficult.' Sometimes, he said, she felt she'd like to go to another church.

He felt aggrieved that the hierarchy had appeared not to be sympathetic or understand the financial problems he had taken on because of having to help his first wife financially. He resented the fact he had to pay for his own uniform. Now life was easier financially, and his second marriage was 'a very different experience'.

This priest had been sent away to boarding school from the age of 7 years, so feeling a sense of attachment appeared vitally important to him.

Another priest had been married before. He said, 'We just grew out of love. I had to battle with my principles. I've always been close friends with my present wife and her children. We are both deeply in love, but I still wonder if I got it wrong. I will have to stand before God one day about it.'

His wife worked full-time in order to pay for housing for when they retire. This meant they had little time together and it was hard for his wife 'who longs to be more involved'. He believed that being a priest had been hard for his children. 'They have had remarks at school.' He also said it was difficult to have close friendships in the parish, because it can cause jealousy.

A priest said his 'second marriage has been great'. His wife had stood by him through a very difficult time when he 'fell in love' a few years earlier. Though that hurt her 'deeply' and he had to move jobs, they were working things out together and amidst all the 'grot' good has come out of it.

The wife of one priest left him five years previously. It had been a total surprise to discover she was having an extra-marital liaison with someone in the church. He had since remarried.

3. The Family within the Marriage

The priest who had described himself earlier as a 'rebellious person' said, 'My family are very proud of me being a priest and value it greatly'. This clergyman, who said he had lost his faith and wasn't sure he should still be in the ordained ministry of the Church of England, said, 'fifteen years ago, I made my family my priority'. He felt his children had been affected when young because they hadn't had his attention. Four years earlier, his wife had been gravely ill. This major crisis had made him think through many issues.

His wife had worked for most of their marriage, which had helped financially. He was cross with the Church, however: 'I have no time for hobbies and it is very difficult to have personal friends because of the hours I work and how all-consuming the work is.' He said that he was an 'introverted person trying to be an extrovert'. Church had dominated his life, though he had a good marriage and his wife supported him: 'We talk endlessly.'

One priest described how it was 'a slow bereavement not being able to have children'. He seemed a sociable man who enjoyed friendships and many hobbies. His wife worked full-time and he said, 'She copes magnificently with parochial life.' For him, friendship and hobbies fed his spirituality.

4. The Working Spouse

The themes of spouses working in order to help the family financially, the priest feeling unable to contribute enough economically, and the children being affected by their ministerial life, were echoed many times throughout this category in the research. Working spouses wanting to develop their careers, and the ways in which this impinged on the general running of the household, were woven in throughout the reports – all encapsulated within the framework of the demands and expectations of parish life, and coping with being at the centre of many people's need.

Some wives said, 'I don't like being called the rector's/vicar's wife' and kicked against being seen as 'belonging to someone' rather than being their own person. Others said they loved the hurly-burly of it all and were very involved. All of them saw being married to a priest as involving some sacrifice. As one priest said, 'The work of a priest has denied me sharing a great deal of quality time with my wife. The job is totally unmanageable, except by devoting an immense amount of time, at the expense of my relationship with my wife.'

Many wives found their husbands forgot to tell them where they were at any given time. 'The parish encroaches all the time, and on that part of me which also belongs to my wife.' As one priest said, 'It is important to get the balance right between family life and parish ministry.' Many clergy had regretted that they had not been more involved at home when the children were younger.

One of the wives was a non stipendiary minister who helped out in her husband's church. He said, 'I share virtually everything with her. She has many roles, and also has to cope with me. I can't imagine how it would be to be married to someone who was not committed to the parish.'

Those spouses who had married someone prior to ordination in a job outside the Church had particular adjustments to make. Not only did they cease to live in a house of their own choosing, but often they were disadvantaged financially because their partner's salary had dropped significantly. These spouses went out to work, often from necessity.

One wife had earned money so that her husband could train for the ministry. Their children were then 13 and 10 years old. 'They found it very hard me changing jobs and training to be ordained. My son detested living in the vicarage and so went away to boarding school.' Though his wife had been supportive she had felt 'let down by the Church and the hierarchy and after much agonising' had left the Church and gone over to the Roman Catholic Church.

One priest had found it hard to find a job in the Church of England. It had been even more difficult for his wife, who still had no job after five years in the parish. They had married later in life and so had no children. He said, 'It is my job that is important, though I have been prepared to go where she is working.' He said he seldom took holidays.

6. The Protective Partner

Two clergy described their wives as 'more than a curate would ever be' and 'a more convinced Christian than I am'.

Two other clergy had wives who were 'very supportive and protective'. They saw it as their role to keep their spouses 'on the rails'. Some of the wives guarded their husbands against the things that get them down or on top of them.

Supportive – Female Clergy Marriages

1. The Shared Family Pain for the Female Priest

Within the samples there were three female clergy, each married. Two had children and one did not. One said that marriage had been very important for her. Her husband had been 'very supportive' from the beginning of training, even though he wasn't then a Christian. He had however, 'been frustrated at times as the Church has infiltrated everything' in their lives. He and the children got angry with what the Church had done to her and to them. They were particularly hurt when people refused to receive the sacraments from her hands because she was a woman. This priest said that her husband still had to be the financial provider.

2. The Supportive Husband

One female priest declared herself 'stressed out by everything'. As she talked more about it, she described her husband as 'a rock, always there' for her. It was her elderly mother who caused her the most stress, as she lived over 200 miles away and needed regular visiting.

The house of this female priest was immaculate, with nothing out of place. She looked neat and well-groomed, but was, however, very stressed and talked about the pressure of life constantly.

Another, who had said her husband was delighted 'not to have to pay a mortgage', said he had given up a job he had disliked. She said: 'Being a priest hasn't affected my marriage at all but I couldn't cope without being married, as it has been a great support.'

Supportive – Homosexual Relationships

One priest described himself as gay. He was in a stable relationship, and though his partner did not live with him he saw him once or twice a week and had been with him for 10 years. The clergy team knew about his partner, though he did not believe the hierarchy were aware. He had not been asked about it. He said, 'I don't talk about it in the parish. I don't feel any need to talk about it. My sexuality is part of me. I believe my personality, sexuality and spirituality are all bound up together. I believe it would cause a problem in the parish among some people, so I don't mention it.'

He went on to explain that he was wary of getting too close to people in the parish because 'people are very needy and they don't understand that friendship is limited by time, and so they get hurt when clergy leave'.

This priest did not readily admit he was in a gay relationship. However, as he talked of his partner it appeared to be a stable and very supportive relationship.

Another single priest talked about the importance of his homosexual relationship. He did not live with his partner of 14 years, though they were in and out of each other's homes. He described the relationship as 'a deep and loving one' which had never weighed him down with guilt. He said he had never hidden the fact he was gay and in a permanent relationship. He was very 'up-front' about it at his Selection Conference and he did not know what the problem was all about. He said: 'My relationship is deeply supportive and we help and respect each other and are not threatened by each other.' He said, 'The Church has not collapsed and they have been ordaining gays for years. If the Church decides not to ordain gay clergy in a relationship, I do wonder if my orders will suddenly be rendered of no value.'

Discussion

All these respondents had recognised the importance of close intimate and supportive relationships. Several had said they could not manage without the backing of their partners. In spite of the cost to the partner's work, home and way of life, all had paid tribute to what had been given up for them. What does this tell us about the psychological needs of these clergy?

Dicks (1967) describes three reasons why people marry:

1. Physical attraction

2. Shared cultural background

3. Unconscious forces

'It is this last named aspect which . . . constitutes the personal psychological core of marital life, not only in the disorders of marriage but also as the healthy, normally functioning element which binds two people in a dyad' (Dicks, 1967, p. 8).

The clergy who have been described above all expressed the importance of their partner's support – some even going so far as to state, 'I don't know what I would do without it.' The fact that some wives 'guard and protect' their husbands and 'keep them on the rails' suggested quite a high degree of dependency. Though 'love requires a partial giving up of personal, selfish demands in order to be able to consider . . . the needs of the loved one . . . it is nevertheless a real loss of . . . freedom' (Skynner, 1976, p. 113).

Whose freedom was lost? In all the cases examined it was the clergy who had been enabled to pursue the path they felt was God's will for them because of the self-sacrifice their partners had seemingly willingly undertaken. They had gained the freedom to follow a particular pathway whilst their spouses had forfeited some of their own freedom. Often the children had made sacrifices as well.

Several of the clergy had been divorced and remarried. Though many reasons were given for the marriage break-up, the inability to cope with the demands of ordained ministry certainly appeared to be a notable one. Maybe the partner's own dependency needs prevented them from allowing their clergy partners to make all the demands.

When candidates come forward to start the process leading up to a Selection Conference, the Diocesan Director of Ordinands (DDO), interviews the candidates and their partners in their own homes several times. There is no requirement that a spouse shares their partner's spiritual beliefs or that they have any desire to see their partner ordained. The interviews are more concerned with the stability of the relationship, and the effect the training and subsequent ordination will have on their family life. If there are concerns, the DDO may well ask the candidate to be interviewed by someone with the ability to discern their psychological integration. However, it is not an easy task to surmise how the relationship itself will cope with the ordained ministry, nor whether the dependency needs of the candidate will produce an intolerable burden on the spouse, potentially leading to the break-up of the marriage.

Some of those interviewed, who had experienced boarding school at an early age and maternal loss and deprivation, found a partner who provided a 'good enough' attachment figure for them to rework the developmental stage they had not negotiated. Those whose first marriages had ended described partners whose needs were greater than their own. Such dependency needs could not be accommodated within the 'goldfish bowl' of parish life.

Kirk and Leary (1994) may be right in asserting that clergy marriages are usually not founded on grand sexual passion. From this research it appeared that the bedrock of a permanent relationship was where the priest could depend on a partner's caring support. It was surely this that enabled the clergy to cope with the vagaries of the modern-day culture more than just depending on their own internal emotional strength and ego identity.

Demanding

There are spouses who seem unable to cope with life as they have to live it. 'The dyad itself has the task of integrating the personal need systems of two (people) . . .' (Dicks, 1967, p. 314). Only two of the clergy were located within the category marked 'demanding'. The following two categories from the data were descriptive of how the clergy presented themselves at interview.

1. The Depressed Couple

One priest said he had been off work for four months because of depression. His wife found parish life very difficult because of the isolation and he felt physically isolated because of the constant vandalism to the vicarage. 'We don't feel we belong and we feel like fish out of water.'

Though this priest said his wife was 'supportive and helpful', it appeared that her need was just as great as his. They lived in a very deprived parish with high unemployment. They dared not leave the house for holidays or days out, because as soon as they did so, windows were broken. Several times tyres had been stolen from their car, and there had been attempts to steal the car itself.

There was a sense of deep hurt invading the whole house. The priest's wife seemed just as depressed as he was. This relationship had the appearance of the 'babes in the wood' which Dicks (1967) describes. All the bad and wicked is located outside and the couple are left huddled together in fear and deep despondency.

The priest described his early life as a lonely one. His parents' marriage was not good, and he was an only child. He did not get married until his late 30s, though they had known each other for nine years before that. They had no children.

There appeared deep cracks of fragmentation within this couple's life. Their main interest was connected with design. Through this interest they had made friends around the world on the Internet. This desire to design, to create, appeared to be a very concrete attempt to be involved in their own inner healing. The experience of such disintegration had the possibility of being woven into a rich tapestry. It may not ever have been possible for this couple to operate in such a demanding environment when their own needs were so obvious.

This priest had already had a period of time outside the ministry, and thereafter it had then been hard for him to find a suitable parish. They had had to leave their previous parish because a female priest had been appointed to work there, and he was unable to accept women priests. Unable to care for her husband, it appeared that the problems his wife experienced only added to his feelings of stress and pressure, thus piling more demands on to him.

2. Shattered Ideals

One priest and his wife went to college with high hopes of being the 'model vicar and vicar's wife'. They found that they didn't fit into college and were not encouraged to work together there: 'College was not easy for us and our first curacy was very difficult as well.' When they arrived in the parish the house had been flooded, the carpets were soaking and there was mildew on the walls. Their son was born two weeks after the priest was ordained. He said that his wife 'would push the pram round the park crying all the time'. He had been unaware of this. During the second curacy his wife had been counselled by the vicar's wife, which had helped a lot.

This couple started out with great expectations of working together for the Lord's sake, but nothing seemed to go right for them. Far from being able to support her husband through training and the first curacy, this wife found it all intolerable. As a result the pressures and demands of study and then ministerial work, on top his wife's needs, crushed all his earlier enthusiasm.

This couple needed the supportive care of an incumbent and his wife in their second parish to nurture them through their pain. Now things were easier: 'My wife feels she doesn't have to be a vicar's wife as she can now be herself. She is now doing things for herself and so is much happier and feels more at home. What she needs most of all is a close friend, which isn't easy in a parish setting.'

Discussion

Though both these couples were from northern parishes, with the attendant increased poverty and unemployment, there was no certainty that they would have fared better in a southern parish. In both situations there seemed to be mitigating circumstances – in one, a lot of violence directed against the church and the vicarage, and in the other an unsatisfactory housing situation. Add to this a sense of disappointment that ministry was not quite what had been envisaged and the husband's deep depression, and it is easy to understand why these two couples appeared not to be coping. For one of them the shared vision ended in disaster.

Many of the clergy couples in the older age group followed a more traditional marriage relationship. Many spouses had been content to stay at home whilst the children were young. However, as they later began to develop their own self-image through embarking on a career, the couple found themselves drifting apart and leading separate lives. It appeared that one couple were in danger of that occurring in their relationship.

Other spouses found their marriage enhanced, however, as they sought extra parochial employment because of all they now brought in concrete terms to the marriage. The clergy husband may have felt he was not contributing enough to the marriage, but if the couple were able to tolerate that, the marriage was enriched.

Some wives, who had faithfully over many years been the traditional clergy wife, felt when their husbands had retired that they had given up everything for him and yet had nothing to show for it. Exploring human growth and development and how each stage is reached and negotiated, as Jacobs (1996) and others do, it is possible to parallel this to different stages in marriages. Whether of short or long duration some marriages will have the appearance of being in the early stages of dependency.

The initially dependent relationship will find it hard to survive if either of the couple begins to develop as individuals. Certainly the couples within this category had the appearance of being within the earlier developmental stage. Though one couple was beginning to separate out, there was a need for quite a bit of adjustment in order for the relationship to remain intact.

Thinking of the needs of Anglican parochial clergy will need to take into account the needs of the spouse as well. The 'crack' may open up if the spouse is unable to tolerate all that is part of the clergy's work package.

Distant

The previous category examined the relationship which appeared demanding. The demanding marriage or partnership can soon become distant if the demands cannot be met. Then one partner will look for someone else, or something else, to fill what may feel like a gap. Ashdown (1998) describes the breakdown of her marriage in graphic detail and the pain and sense of betrayal she suffered. 'If I were to say how it felt, it would be: "I'm breaking up inside. I hurt so badly, I want to run away – so please just leave me alone."' (Ashdown, 1998, p. 31)

The Break-up of the Male Clergy Marriage

The break-up of a marriage for the parochial clergy is a very public affair. There is no way of hiding it from the church congregation when a spouse leaves the vicarage/rectory. Neither is there any possibility of parishioners not eventually finding out if the marriage has broken up because of an extra-marital liaison.

One of the main concerns of the Church hierarchy is to ensure that the press do not get a chance to report yet more salacious scandal. Because of this, bishops issue through their Communications Department a statement about the break-up of the marriage which bears little resemblance to the trauma and anguish of the past months.

Whilst the bishop aims to pastor (and where necessary discipline) a possibly recalcitrant priest, he also appoints a representative, whose role is to provide pastoral and practical help to the deserted spouse. If the priest has left the parsonage house then the spouse has about three months in which to find alternative accommodation for themselves and children, not to mention employment or a source of income. They also have the task of trying to get their life back together again. All of this is acted out in public, and it is almost impossible to keep the grief and pain within the privacy of their home.

There were two priests, one from the north and one from the south, whose wives had left them a few months prior to the interviews. In both cases, when the pilot study questionnaire was sent out, the wives had still been living with their husbands. One priest had telephoned to explain what had happened, wondering if he was still eligible to take part in the research. It was only when questioning the other clergyman about his wife and family that it became clear why the house seemed so neglected and he was chain-smoking.

The other clergy in this category were single, widowed or divorced, though there were two clergy who were married. All, however, appeared 'distant' in relationships – whether friendships or the spouse they lived with.

Bowlby (1973) looks at the problem of aloneness. He traces the need for humans from the beginning of time to be in groups or to have a companion for the sake of physical safety. He believes that that is still a necessity for today. He states that we are 'so constructed that we find comfort in companionship and seek it' (Bowlby, 1973, p. 172). When alone anxiety and despair are often experienced.

Both the clergy whose wives had left them exhibited extreme anxiety and depression. One had said from the pulpit in his sermon, 'God, if you are out there, show yourself.' The other priest had been off work with depression for four months. He said he had been unable to function at all.

This 'interpersonal isolation, generally experienced as loneliness, refers to isolation from other individuals' (Yalom, 1980, p. 353). Though this isolation is about a loss of intimacy, it often becomes an experience of existential isolation, which is 'an unbridgeable gulf between oneself and any other being' (Yalom, 1980, p. 355). The person becomes split off from the rest of the world. A sense of dislocation is then experienced and the loneliness of being totally responsible for one's life. Though this isolation is an experience for everyone, either fleetingly or when people are allowed space in a noisy world to think and reflect, it is nevertheless exaggerated and intensified when disaster strikes, for people are then aware of the fragility of life.

Reasons for the Break-up

One priest had no warning that his wife was leaving. She had gone off with a church member whom they knew socially. He said, 'It has been dreadful and I am having ongoing counselling. I feel it will take at least a year to put myself back together again.' He believed his wife would not come back to him, and said 'She has changed beyond all recognition.'

(a) Lack of Privacy

As he thought about what caused it to happen he said, 'We lived an open-door policy for two years. My wife was a traditional vicar's wife and I felt she and I were very happy, but I've inherited the worst job in the diocese. I knew it when I came.' He then went on to describe how the parish is in terminal decline and bankrupt. Buildings were dilapidated and the team was not functioning. The clergyman said, 'I went off to Evensong and when I came back she had gone and the house looked as though it had been burgled.' This deeply hurting man felt he was just crawling back from the brink.

(b) Lack of Time with the Family and Pressure of Work

Another priest had realised for much longer that his wife was finding being married to him difficult. He had spent very little time with the family when the children were little. Now his wife had a high-powered job and was commuting round the country a lot – 'we hardly saw each other.'

He also came into a very difficult parish situation where there had been five members of staff. One of the non-stipendiary clergy moved and had a 'breakdown' and the other 'caused all the problems of horribleness and had to be asked to leave'. He felt very unsupported by the hierarchy and sensed it was 'all these pressures' that have a lot to do with his wife leaving. 'She just felt she could no longer carry my burdens as well as her own. My going into the ministry put a lot of strain on my wife and she feels that she and I lost the ability to be friends.'

(c) Competing with God

One priest was divorced a few years ago though his wife left several years before. 'My wife felt she was married to a bigamist. My mistress was the Lord. She could never come to terms with God being in my life and could not feel comfortable with my sense of vocation.' He described himself as a workaholic and that his wife 'got more and more resentful. Then there was someone else and she left.' He had never wanted to marry again or have a relationship. He goes on holidays on his own and doesn't have many friends. 'I live for the job and the job lives for me.'

(d) The Supremacy of the Role

Another priest had been married and divorced twice. He said, 'I felt in my first marriage that I had married someone who carried my intelligence. My wife was bitterly opposed to my doing a degree. I had romantic ideas of priesthood and spent hours and hours working though I did help in the house, but my priesthood came first.' His wife became a counsellor and met someone else. His second marriage lasted five years and he wondered why it began, as she had both a drink and a personality problem. He had no desire to be in a relationship again.

(e) Aloneness

Both of the married clergy said their wives found being married to clergy difficult. One wife found the parish 'alien and lonely' as she came from a different part of the country. She felt 'the church culture was bizarre'. Again, this wife was unhappy that he wasn't around more for the children. He said, 'She will not be a vicar's wife. She is her own person and does her own things.' Both wives worked, which had made life more tolerable for them, especially financially.

Female Clergy

A single female priest said, 'I've never felt the desire to be married or have children. I love being alone and go on holiday on my own as I use it as a retreat. I do not feel I need taking care of.'

One priest's husband had died before she started to go to church. It was as a result of his death that she turned to religion. She had started drinking and the curate, who also had a drink problem, came and visited her. As a consequence, she began to find God and eventually went forward to train for the ordained ministry. She said, 'I have very little time for leisure and my children resent the Church, as they feel it has taken me away from them. I'm not good at taking holidays and find it hard to keep up friendships.'

Discussion

All these clergy, for different reasons, had struggled with intimate relationships. Part of the answer for them was to work harder so that they did not have to be vulnerable and fear more rejection in close friendships.

Whatever unconscious forces brought the married couples together, it has been seen that the demands of the job, and the needs of each other, had caused almost intolerable stress. Though 'marriage is always an attempt at growth, at healing oneself and finding oneself again, however disastrously any particular attempt may fail for lack of sufficient understanding or external help' (Skynner, 1976, p. 127), there comes a time for many when it is too painful to look for healing within a relationship.

Balanced

Mutual Support

Ten of the clergy interviewed who were in the above category were single, of whom six were from the northern diocese. During interviews it became clear that the younger clergy from the north, who were modern Catholic by tradition, met regularly. They had become a very supportive group for each other. Partly this was prompted by the ordination of women to the priesthood. The male clergy who had supported women priests had been ostracised by former friends who remained firmly opposed to it. Consequently, this group met frequently and provided a lot of affirmation for each other. It was particularly striking in the light of the fact that the rest of those interviewed appeared to have few, if any, clergy friends and certainly did not meet regularly in groups. As has been stated earlier, the Chapter meetings, are often far from supportive.

These young clergy, some of whom came from deprived backgrounds, had needed to feel 'attached'. As one priest said, 'My childhood was very lonely, as my parents were out at work all day, so I spent a lot of time on my own.' Now he was on his own, he said, 'It has never bothered me that I am on my own. I like my own company and have always had close friends in the parish.' He went on to say that he had 'a strong sense of the life of the world to come and that partings are not permanent.'

Holding such views provided a defence against deep existential isolation. This priest appeared to have some understanding of his own psychology and so had provided a way of coping with the fear of rejection. This provided a sense of balance. His home was warm and decorated in bright colours and he had a house-keeper who looked after all his needs – there was a sense of his being at peace with where he was. He had experienced a mental breakdown as a young man, which will be looked at later. He was aware of his own needs.

Another priest had wished to marry but this had not happened. He described himself as a celibate for whom friendships are very important. He had friends both within the congregation and outside. This intelligent man, who looked after himself, appeared to live in a state of chaos and semi-squalor. Though he had felt badly let down by a Bishop some years previously, he appeared content in where he was now.

One priest said, 'It has never bothered me that I haven't married. I would have liked to but I like my own company.' He came, he said, from a very happy and stable background. As a conservative Evangelical, he had a very definite view of faith and how to live out the Christian life. His family was very supportive and he had a lot of close friends.

Female Clergy

The two female clergy in the category came from the southern diocese. One was single but said, 'I'm not lonely as I have cats and geese.' She believed that her gift was to be single. She had many good friends who were mainly outside the Church. Though she would like to have been able to stay at home for the holidays she cannot do that, as people phone her up wanting something.

Another priest's husband died many years ago. She had no children. Even though she had only been in the parish for two years, she had a very close friend who lived opposite her. She said, 'I find someone to be close friends with in every parish. Here I take holidays with my friend.' One priest found balance and a sense of meaning in her animals, whilst the other priest found it in a friend.

Single Clergy

Two of the clergy admitted to their sexuality being a grey area. For these clergy also, belonging to a supportive group of clergy and having friends they could spend holidays with was very important. One priest said, 'I belong to a company of Mission priests, where we make a vow not to marry as a yearly promise.' This leads to a celibate lifestyle, though he didn't see himself having a strict celibate lifestyle for the rest of his life. 'I have had times of confusion in the past and I don't like living on my own as I miss having someone to talk to.' He found it difficult if he made friends with a non-churchgoer. He said, 'They trespass on our friendship by feeling I won't mind. Though they are letting God down rather than me, I take it very personally.' He had described himself as 'a bit of a loner', but in spite of that, he needed attachment figures to anchor him.

Two other priests stated they would like to marry, but that it would encroach on their freedom and it would be 'a real shock to pick children up from school'. One said, 'I enjoy living on my own. If I got married I would have to sacrifice my space. I'm used to being my own master and making my own decisions on my own.' He had not told any of his close friends about his girlfriend of four years. He believed he was 'a selfish person'. Both clergy were young and at the start of their ministry, and appeared anxious and nervous at the interview, and wanting to impress.

Preparing for Death

The last person in the category was a priest who had had to retire suddenly because of an incurable disease. He was badly disabled and his wife worked. He said, 'We have been planning for my death and how my wife can live her own life in her own way.' She had seen 'priesthood as a large lion leaping through a flaming hoop'. He had found it hard to distinguish between what was work and what was play. He said, 'I have now fewer close friends because of my journey of suffering. When you take up the cross you do it on your own. People can watch and go a certain part of the journey with me; the rest I have to carry on my own.' He had found that this year he had been on his own. Some of his friends had been prepared to stand and watch while others had drifted away and stayed in the background.

Discussion

The difference between this category and the 'demanding and distant' categories was small. In all the categories the clergy came from mixed backgrounds of 'good enough' parenting. It was how they had integrated the pain of the past that appeared to make the difference.

The clergy in this last group were aware of their internal needs and vulnerability. They appeared more cognisant of the cracks in their psychic development and therefore in their adult lives than the other categories. Those in the 'stable marriage' group who needed a supportive spouse seemed to defend against an existential fear of fragmentation. The spouse provided all the 'good enough' mothering that enabled the clergy person to function as an adult in the world.

Within the 'distant and demanding' categories the needs of the spouse were as noticeable as those of the priest. The added pressure of their demands, combined with the strain of the job, often caused a breakdown in their relationships. For some this meant a break up of the marriage, whilst others managed to hold the relationship together through living more separate lives.

Many clergy said that the stress of the job put enormous strain of their personal relationships.

Conclusions

Reasons for Stress

- Many clergy highlighted lack of money as a major cause of stress – financial needs prompted the spouse to work outside the home. The clergy felt inadequate because they could not provide sufficiently for their families.
- Being different and set apart made it difficult to find and keep up friendships.
- Lack of free time often meant little chance of sharing themselves with their families.
- Needs of families, especially when they have young children.
- Expectations of parishioners.

Bowlby, like Freud and others before him, has rightly shown the importance of early attachment figures on adult lives. It is Bowlby, however, who highlights the importance of the emotional attachment in order for the human being to develop mutually conducive adult relationships. Whatever idea the clergy had of their own priesthood, whether representative, pastor, servant or shepherd, it was in the home that their psychological make-up was seen at close quarters and worked out.

The spouse or the priest who felt unheard and unaffirmed, may experience a sense of betrayal. It was when these feelings were unacknowledged that the crack within the relationship became so big that it was past repair. Several of the clergy in the sample had experienced broken marriages and had been divorced. Two clergy were experiencing the immediacy of that pain.

The cracked pot is a reminder that there is the possibility of light shining through the cracks, or the crack itself providing beauty to the whole object. How tolerable these cracks are and how to live with them is the question that the clergy have to wrestle with before there is any possibility of resurrection.

The first hypothesis (see Introduction, page 14) highlights the pressures from without. This chapter has examined whether, given the stress from living in a climate that is alien to what the clergy stand for, the support they receive from those closest to them provides them with the necessary emotional strength to maintain their ministries adequately.

The importance of the role of the partner has also been clearly shown. Where the clergy felt 'attached' to someone who was there for them, they appeared to have a greater degree of internal emotional strength. The research did not explore whether that was solely due to their own internal integration or rather also as a result of the relationships they had.

From this chapter it can be seen that 'the disease within' does affect the whole of their lives, as well as their partner's. The following chapter explores how this is worked out in parish ministry.

Chapter 6: In the driving seat

Leader within the parish

If anyone sets his heart on being an overseer, he deserves a noble task.
Now an overseer must be above reproach . . .
1 Timothy 3:1

Starting work in a new parish produces feelings of excitement, nervousness and apprehension. Usually, the clergy express a feeling that God has called them to this particular work. The words of Frances Ridley Havergal's hymn 'Take my life and let it be consecrated, Lord, to thee', may well express their desires as they start this new ministry at their institution service.

This particular question explores the clergy's leadership style within the parish, as well as how they related to parishioners. In order to do that, the research investigated how training had prepared this group of clergy for ministry; how they handled different people; how they perceived their role; how they coped with sexual advances, or with feeling sexually drawn to someone other than their spouse; how aware they were of dependency needs, both their own and those of others in parochial situations; boundary issues; and awareness of their own denial and defence systems at work. The aim of this section was to highlight the clergy's awareness, or otherwise, of their own vulnerability, and how they managed this. Their feelings about the future of the Church of England were also explored.

Identity

Human beings usually have their own concept of how they would like to be. Certainly clergy seem to have a desire to fulfil a particular model of priesthood, with a particular ministry in the parish.[1] Their psychological health will be affected by whether

---

1 see Chapter 4

they feel they match up to their own ideal. However, their ideal may become a mask as they aim to be what they feel they cannot attain. As they experience the harshness of parochial ministry, their inner vulnerability may not be sufficiently inviolable to defend them from feelings of disintegration.

It has already been noted that the largest percentage of clergy are introverted. They find it extremely difficult to share personal feelings and expose their vulnerability. The idea of being weak is abhorrent to them. Sunday by Sunday they are at the front of the church, leading services, hearing the confessions of the congregations and absolving them, and preaching about a way of life and faith that they feel they themselves must be seen to uphold. It is not surprising that they find it hard to admit to thoughts and feelings they may describe as sin in others, as this would appear to lose them any respect or credibility.

Wives deserted by clergy husbands will say how hard they found it to listen to their husbands preaching what they had not been practising at home. Being deserted by them felt like a massive betrayal – especially as the husband often managed to delude the congregation with the Christian authenticity of his preaching. Not surprisingly, these wives are left full of bitterness.

Splitting

This study, however, is about the clergy and how they manage to live with the internal 'splits', or feelings of fragmentation. 'Splitting' is a term used especially by Klein (1950s) to denote the way the ego is 'split off' from its self. This defence mechanism ensures that the good object is split off from the bad. Parishioners, and clergy themselves, have a need to perceive the priest as wholly good. It is therefore easier for clergy to split off the bad within themselves and project it on to an external object. Many clergy find chairing the Parochial Church Council very difficult, so it is hardly surprising that this body of people often become the enemy.

For some clergy in the research, it was the institution of the Church itself which was the 'bad object'. Having allowed women to be ordained priest, many of the clergy were unable to face their fear of losing dominance and control, and so the women became the split off part of themselves. It was as though the male clergy had allowed women to 'carry' their feminine, or unacceptable side of themselves, and it was hard for them to take back those projections. Other clergy saw their bishops, who became inadequate father figures for them, as the 'bad object'.

Defence and Denial

Defence mechanisms include 'all techniques used by the ego to master, control' (Rycroft, 1968, p. 28). Though the defence system is used to protect the ego, and to play a part in normal development, it may nevertheless receive a severe battering from external and internal forces. Clergy who have suffered deprivation in their families of origin, causing them to have an immature ego, will need a strong defence system. It is in the ministry in the parish with the congregation, and in interaction with the community at large, that clergy feel most vulnerable.

'Many writers have emphasised the lack of self-concern that characterises a religious approach to self-knowledge' (Watts and Williams, 1988, p. 97). Clergy are extremely reticent in looking at themselves. Dioceses that plan therapeutic support groups, or offer an opportunity to look at clergy marriage, find little support and interest. For the clergy, often ministering on their own in the parish, there is a perception that they provide answers. It is extremely embarrassing for many clergy to admit to vulnerability. As one clergyman said, 'I cannot cope with the verse that says, 'When I am weak then I am strong' (2 Corinthians 12:10). He felt he had to wear a mask of confidence and strength continuously. Meeting conflict situations in the parish became a nightmare from which he felt he would never wake up.

Often it is the priest's fear that produces such strong defences, and it is these defences which prevent clergy from being aware of the risks inherent within their profession. Clergy who show warmth and compassion on a funeral visit are seldom aware of the dangers they may run. Often they are unaware that too much intimacy to a bereaved person may send signals of love, rather than just pastoral care. Because of their lack of self-understanding, clergy can find themselves compromised in a situation from which they are completely unable to extricate themselves. Many clergy marriages have broken down because of a lack of insight and naiveté in the face of such need.

'Career counsellors have been saying for years that many of the major difficulties which pastors experience in their work stem from interpersonal problems' (Francis and Jones, 1996, p. 117). Now Bishops are showing concern at the risks their clergy run. Nationally, and in many dioceses, codes of conduct have been devised to ensure the safety of the clergy. All clergy and all laity involved in any way with children must conform to and abide by strict guidelines, both to prevent child abuse, and also to minimise the risk of litigation.

How much are clergy aware of the effect they have on others? They may be seen as parental figures who will meet all the emotional needs of the congregation. Clergy are often seen by the needy as a former object from their childhood. They speak with the authority of God, the 'Father' of all, so it is unsurprising that they then become icons to be worshipped and adored. Because of the clergy's seemingly impenetrable defence system, they are often unaware of all the projections put on to them, let alone the emotional desires. These may be experienced by the clergy as people becoming over-dependent, and seeking more of their time for themselves. Yet often the clergy feel they cannot be harmed because they are doing God's will. This is all the more tragic when the clergy spouse is made aware that what their partner is preaching bears little resemblance to how they are living. The catalogue of disasters within the personal lives of the clergy regaled in the press illustrates this point.

This defence and denial places the clergy in a very vulnerable position. Because they so often lack self-awareness, they are also unaware of the emotional needs of their parishioners. Today many more clergy have been through counselling courses, or have been in therapy themselves. However, too many still remain who have little or no understanding of human psychology. They are therefore unaware of the danger of 'transference' situations into which they place both themselves and those they are ministering to.

Transference

Joseph Breuer, in conjunction with Freud, discovered the phenomenon of 'transference' (1895). They found that material came up during therapy that had little or no bearing on the actual personality of the analyst. Instead, it was about the patient's thoughts, feelings and desires transferred from significant others in their past. This produced both positive and negative transference, so that the analyst became both loved and hated. The more they understood this phenomenon, Freud and others were able to use this to help their patients bring to consciousness deep conflicts buried in the past (1895). It has become a valuable tool in the whole process of psychotherapy.

It can, however, be experienced as a very dangerous phenomenon when not understood by the unwary. Clergy are particularly vulnerable to this – especially since the advent of the Charismatic Renewal Movement.

In the early 1960s there was a renewed interest in the work of the Holy Spirit. Over the next 30 years this affected the different churchmanships within the Anglican Church, Non-conformist Churches and the Roman Catholic Church. One of the results of this new expression of faith was a greater openness of worshippers to each other, and much greater physical contact. Previously Anglicans had sat in their pews, eyes to the front and arms and hands held firmly by their sides. Now they were prepared to look at each other, touch each other, and during the Peace in the Eucharist, even hug each other. This brought a greater joy and relaxation and freedom to many congregations, which is still experienced today.

The negative side of this experience was the ignorance of many church leaders. They had little awareness that touching and hugging emotionally deprived or abused adults may cause extreme transference situations to develop. They were also ignorant of what 'counter-transferential effects' they themselves may experience. It does not seem mere accident that the incidence of clergy marriage breakdown has appeared to increase within the last 30 years, though there is no statistical evidence to support that claim or to link it to the effects of the Charismatic Movement. Marriage breakdown has now risen to one in three in the general population, although because of the Christian view of the sanctity of marriage, clergy are expected to be 'above' such national trends.

Approaches to Ministry

Work relationships

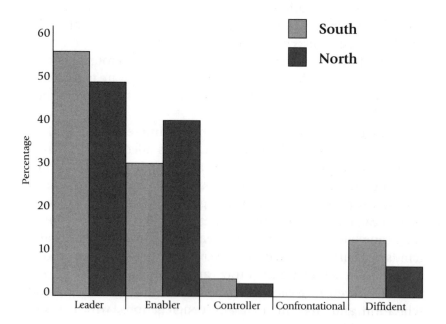

Figure 9

The question exploring the work of the clergy in their parishes addressed these issues. In order to do this, the clergy were grouped under different styles of leadership, as seen in Figure 9, though as with the previous question, this was far from an easy task. The clergy saw themselves as operating different styles of leadership at different times, depending on circumstances. It was their perception of their leadership style, rather than that of their spouse or congregation, that they talked about. It was interesting to note that none of the clergy saw themselves as being confrontational.

These various categories denote what the clergy 'do'. This is about the role of the Incumbent, whereas the question relating to their priesthood was about who they 'are' – about their very 'being'. It could be said that whilst on one level the priesthood is about an internal, almost private role, ministry in the parish is the public, external enactment of the former persona. Some of the clergy bemoaned the fact that people just saw them as the vicar/rector, whilst having no idea what being a priest meant.

When a priest arrives in a parish as the Incumbent, all that parishioners are concerned about, especially the churchwardens, is what their new parish priest will 'do'. Will they help the church to move forward, change things too much, increase giving, or bring more people in? In other words, their underlying desire is for the Incumbent to put the church 'on the map'.

Leadership

Incumbents will have been through a rigorous selection process and training procedure, and then served an apprenticeship curacy. Now they are in sole charge of a parish, under the Bishop, though the remuneration will be small. Living in a consumerist society, the clergy lead congregations largely influenced by materialism. Clergy often live in much larger houses than their parishioners so they have an appearance of wealth without the financial wherewithal to sustain it. The diversity of parishes – country, urban or holiday resort – also causes confusion, e.g. clergy leading a congregation of largely professional, affluent people may

131

themselves have grown up in a working-class environment, or vice versa. It has already been shown that clergy of one churchmanship, operating within a church of another, may find themselves, as well as the congregation, in conflict.

1. Authority

'Leadership gives vision and direction to a group and enables its members to work together to fulfil its aims' (Atkinson and Field, 1996, p. 544). The clergy interviewed expressed these desires. It is, however, difficult to share a vision with a group who are pulling in quite different directions from the leadership. It is equally difficult to work for those whose intelligence is vastly superior to that of the leader – intelligent congregations may find it hard to respect a leader who lacks erudition. How then does it feel to those who are leading from the front? It could be argued that the clergy who had a sense of leading their parishes had a clear identity. Rather than splitting off the bad, these clergy had been able to integrate the positive and negative parts of themselves.

'Leadership' implies power. This power may be based on

- The ability to reward
- The power to punish
- Possessing expertise
- Holding a position of recognised authority
- Attracting and inspiring others.

French and Raven, in Cartwright, ed., *Studies in Social Power*, Ann Arbour, MI, 1959. (Atkinson and Field, 1995, p. 545.)

2. Power

Clergy exert a powerful image. Not only are they dispensers of God's means of grace – the Eucharistic elements of bread and wine – they also hold a universally recognised authority, imparted to them by the bishop. Through enabling others to exercise their gifts, they *reward* their apparent spirituality. The punishment they have power to inflict is to refuse Holy Communion to those who are heretics or are leading immoral lives. The expectation is certainly that they possess expertise in the 'things of God'. To this end it is hoped that they will pray regularly and study the Scriptures, so that they may attract and inspire others to live a godly life. How do the clergy feel they measure up to these criteria, and what effect does this have on their emotional and spiritual needs?

Theological Training

Many of the clergy said that the training they received at college did not prepare them for parish ministry. A 30-year-old priest said that 'the pastoral training was inadequate as it was crammed into three weeks of term, and there was little time to reflect on it and apply it'. Those who went to colleges more in the Anglo-Catholic tradition said they were well grounded in theology, 'had a good knowledge of the Bible and Church history, and learned the discipline of a life of prayer'.

This was especially true for two of the clergy, who had spent time in a monastery. These Modern Catholic clergy were well served by their colleges in priestly formation. They felt, however, that they had not been prepared for the cut and thrust of parochial life. One of them said, 'I came out of college with a very clear idea of what sort of sacrificial pastor/priest I would be – I said Mass beautifully. The college trained introverts to cope and have a sacred space, but I have real problems with people who don't agree with me. A priest and a vicar are different. I can't see why a lay person can't be a vicar, as many tasks of the incumbent aren't strictly priestly.' This clergyman was between the 36-45 age bracket and had been ordained for 17 years.

Clergy of a central churchmanship felt they had fared no better. One priest said, 'College taught me how to drink sherry and play croquet.' Two felt they had not been given any management training. One younger priest said he would have liked a job description from the parish, so that he could know whether he was fulfilling his contract.

Clergy who had come into the ordained ministry later in life after following a career in secular employment brought with them a diversity of experience. One said, 'I got a real picture of how people live in National Service.' He said, 'At my very conservative, evangelical college I was not prepared for ministry, as real life didn't enter into it, so I was very grateful I had been in National Service.'

Those who had attended one of the more evangelical colleges felt they had received very good training in pastoral care and counselling, though less adequate help in sustaining their own spirituality. No one felt they had been taught how to deal with diocesan committees.

Apart from these criticisms, most of the clergy greatly valued their time in college. Those with little previous education received invaluable theological training, whilst for many it was a time set aside to think about what God wanted them to become and do.

In spite of the variations, and both the positive and negative feelings expressed about their training, all the clergy felt that was only one part of the training for ordained ministry. 'Most of the training occurs in the first parish where I trained as a curate.'

The Curacy

Each of those interviewed expressed the importance of their first curacy.[1] It appeared to colour their whole view of later ministry. One priest said, 'You need two curacies with good training incumbents to learn the job well.' He felt it was important to give people the right sort of background. 'At college I was not taught about mission theology, or how to do baptisms and marriages. In my curacies I was given a lot of hands-on experience.' The importance of the training incumbent was expressed repeatedly – several said, 'I owe so much to my first vicar. I learned so much from him.'

In this category only one priest had anything negative to say

---

1 The first 3-4 years are served under a training incumbent as a curate

about the curacy. He said, 'I had a very good first curacy for nearly two years, then the vicar left. I was on my own for four months and then had a difficult nine months with the new vicar.' A senior cleric said that those clergy who had experienced negative or abusive relationships with their training incumbents, would repeat that pattern when they became training incumbents themselves. There is a need for the curate to have a good relationship with their incumbent if they are in time to become good training incumbents themselves.

The various leadership styles now examined come from the material presented by the clergy.

Leader

1. Being 'Myself'

One priest believed that priests could be too holy and unworldly. He saw leadership as about being 'himself'. 'Most people see me as approachable and amiable. I like to be in the community with schools, pubs and shops. The Church is part of the whole package, even if people don't come to church and see me as a total irrelevance. Most people have no idea what vicars do.'

2. The Organiser

Another priest said, 'I can say "no" to people. I am a highly organised priest, and work to calendars and programmes. I have budgets and goals, and I like to plan long-term. I set boundaries and commitments.' If he saw people for counselling it was for one hour, with his wife in the house. He found it hard to cope with those who held fundamentalist views about anything, and believed the moral ground has moved. 'I am a modern person and have kept up to date. I like to see the Church at the forefront of change, and this parish is a liturgically experimenting parish.'

He had definite ideas, and appeared to find it hard to tolerate firm ideas that were opposed to his. He needed clear boundaries to provide a secure holding for himself. It was as though he led from the front so that he would not be able to experience the fear of being out of control. This priest held a science degree, in which there appeared more chance of keeping everything in order. His greatest anxiety was that he could never complete anything. 'I go to bed every night of the week with things left undone. I don't know what it's like to go to bed having completed a task.'

3. The Inflexible Theologian

One vicar said, 'As a leader I need a robust and sustainable spirituality. My relationship to God must be healthy. I need to think theologically so I can bring a theological perspective to bear on what we do in church.' Again this priest stated, 'I find it hard to cope with people whose views are diametrically opposed to mine. I find it hard to get on with those in Forward in Faith, as I don't believe they have any theological ground to oppose the ordination of women to priesthood.' He found people like himself difficult to cope with. 'I am often very quick to jump in on things, and certain people drive me to a frazzle.'

This bright, rather tense man talked incessantly throughout the interview, with no space between to reflect on the questions. Being a training incumbent and a Rural Dean, he felt the only way to manage was to have a tight hold on everything. He also seemed restless, and was not sure he wanted to stay in parochial ministry.

He had a very clear sense of boundary management with people and children. He would take someone else with him to see a woman at night. If someone was sexually attracted to him as happened once, he would set his wife on them. 'If I was attracted to someone I would withdraw and would never be alone with them.' It sounded as though he would be unable to cope with an importunate female without the 'guard dog' qualities of his wife.

4. The Visionary

A priest said, 'When I'm around, things change. I have confidence in the power of the Holy Spirit to get things done. I have confidence we will build a new hospital in four years. I can hold goals for a very long time and I can hold a goal in mind for 17 to 18 years and get it done.' He continued to say that he could speak at 'the drop of a hat' and was able to listen to people. The people he found it hard to cope with were 'the righteous people who won't listen through ignorance or prejudice'. He said he found career clergy very difficult to cope with 'as they posed as holy men and very priestly, while committing adultery with their parishioners'.

He was very clear about managing boundaries: 'I will not transgress and go over boundaries in personal relationships.' Counselling training had made him very conscious of trans-ference and especially if he was dealing with marriage problems. 'I lay down the ground rules very clearly and make sure the person never gets between me and my family.' He acknowledged how flattering it was to receive people's confidence and love, but kept the relationship within the bounds of friendship only.

5. The Diplomat

Those clergy within the category of the Leader appeared to have a clear sense of who they were, and what they were aiming to achieve. One priest said, 'Priests need tact, diplomacy, flair for liturgy, administrative gifts, pastoral gifts and the ability to listen. I try not to reject people. It helps me that I have such a stable and happy marriage, as it prevents me from falling into temptation.' He found however, that boundary management was difficult as there were times when he needed to see people on their own because of confidentiality. He believed that he must not turn people away: 'I believe it is a real strength that people can come and talk without things being written down.' He found thinking through moral issues very challenging, as he had to discover new insights. He said, 'I will back off if people get too dependent. I would not notice if someone was sexually attracted to me, but I think my wife would notice, so I could discuss it with her.'

This clergyman's greatest sadness was that people wouldn't talk to him about their faith. He did not really feel he had the luxury of time for small talk, as he wanted to get on with what he saw ministry to be about.

6. A Manager of Conflict

One of the gay priests said, 'I need to be unafraid of conflict. I believe I have a secure sense of self and a growing spirituality. I do believe we are entering a new Dark Age in the Church of England, as many parishes will never have a priest again. I would like to see the large and small congregations as beacons of light. I do believe the homosexual issue could sink the Church.' This priest had learnt to say 'no' and believed he had to have clear boundaries within relationships in the parish.

7. A Manager of Boundaries

Several of the clergy felt leading the parish involved loving people and accepting them as they are. They had clear ideas of boundary management. Whilst they admitted they may well become sexually attracted to people they are ministering to (and did), nevertheless the relationship must be kept within appropriate guidelines. Many of them felt their spouse would provide the protection needed, either through being available in the house or at work. They felt that sharing the problem with their partner would prevent the situation escalating out of control.

Some of the clergy said they would share any unwarranted attention from others with their churchwardens. If it was their own problem, they would seek out a close friend to share it with. Even if they did not believe sexual attraction to anyone other than their spouse was a problem for them, all the clergy were aware that it was and is a growing problem in the Church. They spoke of those, often within their own Deaneries or known to them, who had had extra-marital affairs and had therefore been forced to leave their parishes.

One such priest said, 'People trust the clergy and expect them to be part of their lives in a more personal way than other professionals. It is a privilege to go into people's homes, and at times I do need to be alone with people, but we must be careful as there is great scope for abuse both ways.'

8. Authoritarian

One priest had 'developed a pastoral ministry to some quite needy people.' He admitted, 'Some people find me bossy, rude, a controller and noisy, and are frightened of me. I do find it hard to work with whinging people and those who try to tell me what I should be doing. I get angry if I feel I am manipulated.' This priest wondered why he had not been given a senior position, appearing not to link this to his lack of tolerance for others. He believed he kept in control of himself. He was once sexually attracted to someone, and talked it out with them. After that it was no longer an issue.

This priest believed the Church of England had become increasingly marginalised, and the clergy also, so that the priest was no longer the person people turned to. He found it depressing that 'clergy do less pastoral work and just keep the handles of the Church turning'.

9. Others First

Another priest had taken his model of leadership from the Army. 'I was trained to put the men first – see that they are fed first, then I could feed myself. If I am going to ask someone to do something I need to know I can do it as well. People see me as a leader, excitable, someone who puts his foot in it, who says sorry, is a pragmatist and who makes every event an occasion.'

He had taken part in a Myers Briggs personality type workshop based on Jung's personality types. Unusually for a priest, he had come out as an extrovert. He said that in church he kissed a lot of women, but he did it to everyone. 'I would be very surprised if anyone was sexually attracted to me, though I am often attracted to women. I find many of them very attractive.' He did say he would be very careful to avoid any compromising situations.

Discussion

Clergy who were leaders within their parish often exhibited a firmness in thought and demeanour. They appeared to know what they wanted and where they were going. Nearly all of them were able to cope with the over-demanding by saying 'no', or recognising that they were unable to meet everyone's needs. Self-knowledge appeared to be very important, as did also knowing their own sexual limitations.

Because many dioceses have recently implemented codes of practice in working with children, the clergy were already alerted to the need for clear boundaries. Those who found such constraints difficult appeared very aware of the dangers inherent in not having a healthy wariness in relationships to others.

Listening and communicating were skills the clergy prized as the 'doing' skills needed to assist the 'being' skill of the priest. All of them echoed in different ways a priest who said, 'I feel like a lump of butter spread too thinly over a fairly large slice of bread.' Even so, he added, 'Christ needs leaders who expect God to do things.' He said, 'People's appetite for my time is insatiable.'

Some clergy from this category saw the healing ministry as an important part of their leadership. One priest who had been involved with the Charismatic Movement said, 'The Church is getting too superficial. Training is inadequate and we are not critical enough of the world, which is getting too secular. I blame the hierarchy as they are the shop window of the Church and they have lost their cutting edge. Clergy are too thinly spread around and I want the Church to remain God's Church and not the people's Church.' This came from an older clergyman who felt he had not been able to mould himself into modern ways.

Single clergy seemed to have different problems from those in relationships. They became easy targets for lonely and single people in the congregations. One priest said, 'I have to be careful, as a widow woman keeps phoning me up. Often I have had to tell people to go and see someone else.' He had a housekeeper, which meant he was never on his own in the vicarage when seeing people.

The hardest thing for this young priest was that he felt very depressed about the split in the Church of England, and especially in the Catholic movement. He said, 'I'm not sure where I am now with my friends in Forward in Faith. I don't feel they are asking the right questions.'

Another priest shared these concerns but added, 'I'm worried more Evangelicals and Liberals are being ordained. I believe the balance in the Church has been lost because of Forward in Faith.'

Conclusion

The clergy did not see themselves in isolation from the rest of the Church. It mattered very much to them what was happening to the institution of the Church. They felt affected by motions passed at General Synod, and pronouncements by Bishops that appeared to cause splits within the institution. It felt unsafe.

About half of the clergy interviewed expressed concern about the Church and its long-term future. The rest felt it was exciting to be part of the Church with so much change taking place. Some said that 'it would not matter if the Church of England died as God would raise something else up to take its place'.

Many of the older clergy found the changes difficult, especially those who had been ordained for a long time. One clergyman said, 'I feel betrayed by the House of Bishops. I look to them to provide moral guidance and they don't. They're no help at all. They don't take a moral stand on abortion and homosexuality. People in the parish ask questions about why the Church does not give a clear lead'.

One of the questions looked at whether the clergy felt overwhelmed by people's needs. Those who had been in ministry for many years felt they did not, whilst those who were younger and had been ordained for less years admitted to times when others' grief had overwhelmed them. One clergyman said, 'I have a heroic view of being a priest. Two of my favourite saints were Jesuit missionaries who were very zealous – fasting, visiting, praying and winning souls – but I have been overwhelmed by people's needs when they've got attached to me and not to Christ'.

He was a young priest who found situations in ministry 'quite scary'. Listening to him talking about his work in the parish it seemed that though he offered a confident front he was, as he said, 'muddling through'.

There was only one woman priest in this category who

appeared to see her role in the parish as leading. She said, 'I am prepared to rebuke people and lead them out of the errors of their ways. As incumbent I have been given the cure of souls.' She believed, as a single woman, she was 'fair game' for people's misunderstanding. She said, 'I would be very upset if people said I was sleeping with a male or a female who happened to be staying in my house.' She was aware that she didn't have a private life. 'I do not like aggressive males and the Church is full of them, and pompous people, and I can get tense and then I need to withdraw.' She said she was not a confrontational person, though she had clear boundaries.

The clergy in this category appeared to have fairly integrated identities. They had a clear sense of who they were, what they wanted out of life and what they believed God wanted with them. They appeared confident in their role as vicar/priest and were prepared to exercise that role, at times forcefully.

It might be expected that those who saw their priestly role as a representative one may be those who also saw themselves as leading the congregation. However, that is not borne out by the statistics. Many representative priests saw themselves as enablers in the leadership style, whilst those who would call themselves pastors appeared to give firm leadership to their congregations.

Enabler

'Enable . . . give (a person, etc.) the means or authority to do something' (*The Concise Oxford Dictionary*, 1990). During the twentieth century there has been much written about empowering people. Beginning with the campaign for women to be given the vote at the beginning of the twentieth century, the emphasis now, as a new century begins, is on equal opportunities for all. Whether it is about seeing women ordained to the priesthood alongside men, or gay rights, any minority group is banging the drum of 'empowerment'.

Whereas in the previous category, 'Leader', the clergy appeared clear that theirs was the public guiding role, envisioning as well as teaching and preparing others, this category is different. Here it seemed the clergy strove to empower their own people, to enable them to find out their gifts and take on leadership roles both within and outside the Church. They were concerned to promote lay leadership, seeing it as being of equal importance to the ordained leadership.

Is it more stressful to hold all the leadership in one pair of hands or to delegate it? Those who prefer the former would have to defend against their own internal cracks. Several clergy said how difficult they found those people who had a very different view from their own. Boundary management was important, not just out of propriety but in order to defend against their own vulnerability and to maintain a safe distance. Those who see their role as one of enabler will, by definition, be more intimately alongside people – a risky business.

1. Ministry of Encouragement

One priest said, 'I let things happen. I don't force anything. I have a modest degree of discernment.' A priest trained in psychology and human growth and development at college said, 'People see me as approachable. I am less judgemental than I used to be and I am seen to have a ministry of encouragement.' Even so, many of the clergy empowered others from their own weakness.

2. Facilitator

A female priest said, 'I get feedback from the bishop and others that I am abrupt. I'm a 'leaping-in' sort of person. Maybe I'm abrupt as a defence against any sort of attack. The Church hasn't really helped as I can feel sorry for myself if people expect too much of me.' She felt, however, that she had changed and was changing. 'I used to be very black and white and allowed my piety to box people up. I had to know I was in control. I had separated out my sexuality from my spirituality and I needed the structures of the Church to keep me safe.' Now she felt she was more mature and able to be kind and accepting. She saw her role as 'teaching and enabling people to take responsibility'.

Though she admitted she would enjoy someone being sexually

attracted to her, she felt she knew how to maintain appropriate boundaries. The fact that she had a good sexual relationship within her marriage had helped her to cope when she had felt attracted to others.

3. Journeying Alongside Others

One priest rode a motorbike 'in order to switch off'. This priest described himself 'as very vulnerable and exposed', especially when wearing a dog collar. 'I won't wear it outside the parish.' Enjoying such a pastime may have acted as a defence against the exposing role he offered as a priest.

He believed a priest needed 'gifts of openness, tenacity, vision and a Godlike sense of humour'. His ministry was about 'dealing face to face with people'. He would take other people along with him when visiting in order to train them. Sometimes he felt excited by the Church of England and felt energised by all the change going on. At other times he was depressed because he feared the Church would not change, and would become irrelevant and an embarrassment. He believed the Church 'needs to be people-focused and to build up the people of God'. He was against building up the hierarchy.

He said, 'It is an awe-inspiring time being with someone when they've just learned they've got cancer and have said they want me there when they die. Also, the time when a baby was born with fatal problems.'

4. Training Others for Ministry

Several clergy saw their ministry as giving people space and encouragement to develop their gifts and so make the contributions that they can. One priest said, 'It is a privilege to be a priest and a joy to be in a position to talk to people about spiritual things.' He said he was less judgemental than he used to be, though he would want 'to take a biblical line on morality'. He believed in preparing people for leadership.

This priest had a very difficult curacy. His training incumbent had been a very able man: 'He thought if I couldn't do what he could do, I wasn't up to the job. I felt very inadequate. It was a very unhappy time.' He described himself as 'a closed man' who doesn't easily open up – yet he did do so in the interview, openly admitting his failures.

5. Collaborative Ministry

Several in this category stated that their theological training did not equip them for working in a parish. One said, 'The pastoral side of ministry is very important. I believe in collaborative ministry. I have wonderful people in church who do pastoral visiting and administrative work on behalf of the church. I try and teach people that we are all involved in ministry. I am able to say to people "I can't do something."' He described himself as a very tactile person who would put his arm around everyone. He did, however, maintain careful boundaries and at all times tried 'to maintain Christian values and standards'. He believed society was post-Christian.

A conservative Evangelical wanted the mystique of the priest-hood to be taken away. 'I want to be seen as a straightforward person. I believe people have created too many barriers between me and them because I'm a priest, so I have been knocking the barriers down.' He believed the traditional values of morality the Church had stood for in the past were more important than ever, 'but I have to meet people where they are'.

This priest had a difficult curacy as the vicar had moved on only three weeks after he was ordained. He was left to 'run' the church for a whole year on his own.

6. The Carer

Some of the clergy saw their ministry mainly within the whole parish so that, as one priest said, 'I live a social gospel.' He was involved in many concerns of the community from Age Concern to the town council. He said, 'I get on with everyone and as I'm out and about I say "Hello" to everyone.' He got more passionate about social injustice than about people's changing moral attitudes.

Four female clergy were in the enabling category. Without gender stereotyping, it is interesting to speculate whether female clergy are more used to enabling others than male clergy. One said, 'I have compassion and discernment. It has helped being a mum.' Another believed experience of life helps. 'I need to be kind, sympathetic and available,' she said. 'Though a leader, I need to enable others to take responsibility for themselves.' This female priest said, 'I have found that women don't really like another woman in leadership. I have three very strong and arrogant women in one church, and I don't handle stroppy people well.' She felt very sad at the divisions in the Church over the ordination of women.

One priest believed suffering is part of being a priest. He said, 'I feel it is important to be empathic. The call to ministry is about taking up the cross.' This priest found it very difficult when people did not like him, avoiding rows and confrontation. He felt his training did not prepare him for parish ministry. This priest appeared to be angry and hurting. At every question he seemed to need to say how wrong the Church was for ordaining women. Having come into the Church looking for affirmation and security, he felt let down by the Church. Though trying to enable others, he appeared disorientated and said, 'I am unsure where I am going because of the women's issue.'

Discussion

Some of these clergy enabled their parishioners to find their own gifts and use them. They did this from a strong internal identity where they appeared able to meet people where they were. Having experienced pain in their own lives, and daring to face their own vulnerability, they had no need to hide behind a mask of leadership. However, other clergy ministered from weakness. It was not something they had worked through but were living through at the time of the interview. The priest whose wife had recently walked out was now enabling others to care for him. Whereas previously he had kept aloof from people and shared nothing of himself, of necessity he was no longer able to hold the mask in place. As a result he admitted that this was a 'healing process', allowing others to care for him. His very vulnerability he began to see as a tool for closer relationships.

These hurting clergy who felt 'let down by the Church' turned in their despair to their congregations for help. The parish church, as represented by the people, became the matrix cradling the wounded priests.

Controlling

It has already been noted that none of the clergy perceived themselves as exercising a confrontational style of leadership. Indeed, several of the clergy stated they did not enjoy confrontation and actually 'ran away from it'. Yet such a public ministry inevitably will attract conflict. Parochial Church Council meetings are often arenas for the disaffected of the Church to state their grievances loudly and clearly. Members, however committed as Christians, have little compunction in telling the present Incumbent that their predecessors managed the parish far more successfully than they do. Many a meeting is prevented from forward planning by such statements as, 'Oh, it was tried 30 years ago and it didn't work then', or, 'We've always done it that way and can't possibly change things now'. Eager clergy arriving with vision and enthusiasm have found themselves annihilated by such attitudes.

Though none of the clergy admitted to using a confrontational style, there was nonetheless enough anecdotal evidence to suggest that there were clergy ministering in Church of England parishes who were exceedingly confrontational. Those who have experienced an irate priest when asking for baptism, wedding or funeral services to be conducted in a particular way do not forget. Because clergy are like others in every area of life, there will be those who are gentle and those who are dominant. Why then did no one in the sample admit to such strong feelings?

It may be that biblical injunction urges against a confrontational style. Many biblical figures are powerful people who thunder out their message – St Paul is one of them. However, he urges upon his readers a gentle style. 'As God's chosen people, holy and dearly loved, clothe yourselves with compassion, kindness, humanity, gentleness and patience. Bear with each other and forgive whatever grievances you have against one another' (Colossians 3:12-13). This message of love is a powerful deterrent against conflict, coming as it does after Jesus' powerful message in the Gospels 'to love one another'.

Some of those clergy may well have been dominant, but unaware of their own confrontational style, though one did admit to being 'bossy and rude'. It was hard for any of them to admit they were invariably confrontational, and such a possibility may well not equate with their own image of themselves.

If not confrontational, were they controlling? This need to control is laid down during an early stage of development. It is difficult to admit to being controlling, as that can sound very manipulative. The clergy who led their congregations often appeared controlling as they shared their vision and ideas with people. They did not, however, seem to take this control to extremes. Control is a defence which provides a false sense of security. Looking through the sample, only two of the clergy seemed to fit this category.

1. Controls against Emotional Interaction

One priest had said that coming into the ordained ministry was for her a way of avoiding real life: 'I felt I could create my own life as I was less likely to make mistakes.' This female priest had grown up in a vicarage 'so knew the score. It felt safe.' For her the world had seemed strange and alien as she 'had never had any contact with anyone in the world'. Because of her mother's verbal violence to her as a child, it was not surprising that she now employed logic and reason in every situation. She said, 'I can't cope with feely-feely people. They find my logical mind difficult. I mustn't be emotionally tied up with people because I may need to rebuke them.' She felt no one would be sexually attracted to her, and if they were she would suggest they went to another church. She said, 'If I was sexually attracted to someone I would move, as it would interfere with my work.' She described herself as very liberal in her thinking about morality, though she believed in commitment and responsibility. She said, 'I am able to step in and out of different thought worlds, and work within their framework.' It was not surprising that this very controlling priest prepared services meticulously.

The interview was not easy as she gave nothing of herself. She appeared very happy in her work and self-sufficient. It was even difficult to get into the front of her vicarage because of the closed five-barred gates. It was like a strong metaphor for her high defences, which had been built up from an early age.

2. Controlling in Order to Survive

The other priest also came from a very difficult background. He described his father as 'a strict authoritarian' and that his parents 'were hooked on duty'. 'I felt cheated out of any emotional input from them. They never took any interest in the school I went to and never came to anything.' Though he said his early childhood was happy, he described his mother as manipulative. His parents had opposed him being ordained and his mother said that he was ruining his life. Because she treated him like a 5-year-old he said he wouldn't speak to her again, and he kept his word. He did not go and see her when she died. Not only were his parental relationships very traumatic, but he had been married and divorced twice. He no longer saw his children.

At interview this priest appeared depressed. He was slow and ponderous in his speech. Even so, he seemed a rather ruthless man who, though talking about forgiveness, was unable to extend that to his parents and to his children. He said, 'I have strict rules about boundary management even though I come over as easygoing. I came from college thinking I was going to convert the world and everyone would toe the line, but in the parish my beliefs went out of the window as I began to work with people who were struggling against the odds. I began to see how courageous people are, and that often what I said was not helpful.' He went on to say that he found people who lie very difficult, and there were times when he took control of situations. He wouldn't allow people to make too many demands on him.

He was aware that if people were sexually attracted to him it

149

was, in fact, 'to the dog-collar and their image of what it is'. He went on to say it was one of the contributing factors to the break-up of his first marriage. Someone was attracted to him and because he stopped going to her house 'she created havoc'. If he felt attracted to someone he would just acknowledge it and then do nothing about it.

This priest had worked in some very deprived areas of London. He knew what it was to be deprived himself and had experienced at first hand the need to survive. Controlling the environment was about survival for this man. As he talked it was as though he was describing a creative controlling, rather than a manipulative way of working. Having had some training in family therapy, it seemed that not only was he prepared to address others' needs, but also to attempt, at least, to understand his own.

Discussion

This priest believed the Church of England 'is putting its house in order pastorally in its concern for clergy'. He believed the institution had the courage to tackle hard issues like gay priests and women's ordination and not to take 'a hard line'. Talking to this priest felt like talking to a battle-weary veteran. Unlike the previous female priest, whose house seemed 'guarded' against intruders and was immaculate, his home was lived in. He had already been battered from within and without and appeared to be using his scars for others, whereas the female priest, having been 'battered' as a child, was determined that would never happen to her again if possible. Clergy who controlled their lives in order to survive seemed aware that this need began in a dysfunctional childhood.

Some clergy needed answers logically worked out in order to make everything safe. Control seemed a negative force for them whilst for others it appeared a creative way in which to cope with the demands of the work.

Diffident

Several of the clergy expressed their fear of leading from the front, of making decisions, and of facing conflict. They appeared anxious and distrustful in their handling of people, and very unsure of themselves in their public role.

Freud was particularly interested in the study of neurotic anxiety. There appears to be no obvious reason for alarm from the external world and yet the person exhibits a profound state of anxiety. Freud believed that this state of anxiety had its genesis in the act of birth and the separation of the baby from its mother. In studying the clergy under this category, it was noted that their 'anxiety always foresees the most frightful of all possibilities, (they) interpret every chance event as a premonition of evil and exploit every uncertainty in a bad sense' (Freud, 1976, p. 446).

1. Programmed to Please

One priest said, 'I don't like confrontational people as I am programmed to please.' He said, 'I hate rudeness, and where people are two-faced and say things behind my back.' Throughout the interview he appeared anxious. At just over 30 years old he seemed younger than his age. He openly shared his fear of becoming depressed. He described his childhood as happy, though he hated his sisters for long periods and fought with them, and he could remember bad times at home.

In rereading the transcript it appeared that he was very anxious to assure himself that he had a happy childhood, even though his parents 'argued at times'. There were some highly important parental figures in his life, such as his school chaplain and his grandmother.

In discussing his work he said, 'The friendships I made at college are very important to me. They give me security.' He was in his first parish as an incumbent and felt he had been 'thrown in at the deep end'. He said, 'I cannot lay down the law to people who don't share my faith, so I am liberal in my preaching on moral issues. I don't give a lead on sexual morals as I don't believe the church is here primarily as a moral institution.' He believed his job was to talk about God's love. He was very worried about what was happening within the Church of England, though he was happy that women had been ordained. He was concerned about the Forward in Faith movement and the strength of Evangelicals. He believed the Church should be a balanced Church. He said, 'I could see myself leaving the Church to become a Roman Catholic.' The Roman Catholic Church provides even stronger boundaries than the Anglican Church.

The psychological needs of this priest seemed to be about safe and clear structures that are a defence against his anxiety.

2. An Avoider

Another priest said, 'I have a low opinion of myself and so would find it astonishing if anyone was sexually attracted to me. I avoid situations where people become dependent. I have never had an awkward encounter, but I am very uneasy when I know members of the congregation are having an affair.'

This young priest appeared slow thinking and seemed to have difficulties in answering the questions. Before the interview he had had a very stressful week baptising a dead baby and then conducting the funeral. He described himself as overwhelmed by mental illness, and said, 'I won't get involved and so I leave it to the professionals. I just do what I feel I can cope with.'

He had struggled with verbal bullying at school. He did not tell his parents as they 'struggled with each other'. He had tried 'to do what is correct'. He and his wife struggled at college when they realised their rather idealised picture of ministry was not the reality. He had a fear of not getting things right and so was ruled by this deep anxiety. It did not allow him to step out of line or to think creatively. It was almost as though his anxiety was like a straitjacket that prevented him flying away.

3. Isolated

One priest was depressed and unwell when the interview took place. His early traumas, due to his parents' divorce when he was 7 years old, had profoundly coloured his life. Coupled with his divorce from his first wife, both had produced what he described as 'an awful lot of darkness'.

He had found help through the Jungian training he had

done. However, he appeared a very fragile, hurting man. 'I'm remote to people and I don't let people bond with me. People can get very dependent, so I work like a therapist and keep to time with people.' He described how at college the talk was about 'the pain in the mind of the priest'. Because he could not offer several sessions of counselling to people, pastoral care was trivialised so he didn't do much of it. 'My wife doesn't like me being out morning, afternoon and evening.' He talked a lot about his shadow side and how he doesn't let other people's needs overwhelm him.

4. Alienated

Another priest said his mother thought that religion was a crutch. 'She was against me getting ordained.' He fought against the training as he didn't fit into the ethos of the college. He went on to say, 'For 95 per cent of the people, what I stand for is an irrelevance, and that affects me. The values I stand for are ignored but I try to build bridges, but I am very defensive about it. I do get depressed about it all.'

This man was anxious throughout the interview. He talked a great deal and it was hard to keep him to the questions. He appeared very real as he shared his struggles with God, as God was not doing what he promised to do. 'I make it clear to people who demand too much of me that I am extremely fallible and I can't meet their expectations.'

One priest was opposed to the ordination of women to the priesthood. Because of his depression he did not easily fit into any category. At the time of the interview he was unable to exercise a 'leading' role. He said, 'The college training didn't prepare me for ministry at all, as it has changed drastically over the past 25 years. I believe one needs enormous resilience and perception in order to bring a spiritual awareness into people's lives. I try to be tolerant with demanding people.'

This priest was very worried about the Church of England. 'The prime issue is the woman's vote and the Church looking backwards. It is not cohesive. Clergy numbers are down and they are under increasing pressure.' He couldn't enable anyone else to find a role, as he appeared to feel he had lost his. There was a sense of real disintegration.

There was one female priest in this category. She was a widow without children. She said, 'People do not feel I am as accessible as I ought to be. As people don't like to upset me, complaints go to the churchwardens. Having three parishes to run, I feel at times I am skating over the surface.' She found young people difficult and did not pop in to the various village groups. She found socialising difficult and after Sunday services she just wanted to collapse and be on her own. She said, 'The computer age is making me very alarmed. I feel I am being left behind.'

Discussion

It was the clergy from the southern diocese who spoke of the Church and the clergy as being an irrelevance. Though people in the north did not appear to attend church any more regularly or in greater numbers than in the south, the Church was seen to be part of the community and therefore important – especially for occasional offices. In the south, people were more likely to opt for civic wedding services, and arrange the funerals of their relatives without the presence of clergy, than was the case in the north.

Looking at the clergy within this category, certain elements stand out. None of them appeared confident of their own ability to lead their congregations forward, and none expressed any vision they may have had. All appeared fearful and hesitant about getting too involved with people. There appeared a clear connection between early childhood deprivation, later breakdown of adult intimate relationships and present-day difficulties with relating within the parish. It was not surprising that symptoms of neurotic anxiety were discernible.

Conclusion

Being a priest is internal. It is how the clergy feel about themselves, which is expressed in their priestly persona. However, being a vicar/rector is public. It is to do with how others see them, and more than that, it affects others as well – community, congregation and the wider Church. It is often not possible to hide feelings of fragility and incompetence. If clergy find themselves near a parish that appears to be thriving, their feelings of inadequacy are multiplied as they are made more aware of their own 'failure'. Low numbers at service, combined with people from their parish attending the more 'successful' churches, exacerbates the problem.

Out of the whole sample, the greatest percentages of priests seemed to cope with the public role they had to enact. The small percentage who struggled are like many in the wider Church, expressing overtly what the others experience at different times in their ministry. The question to be addressed must be, how can the needs of the clergy be met before they reach the degree of brokenness highlighted in the last category?

It is in their public role that the clergy's emotional strengths and weaknesses are exposed, so that the validity of the second hypothesis is underlined. This, then, relates directly to their reaction to modern-day culture.

Chapter 7: The cracked pot

Emotional and spiritual health

Life is about contrasts and opposites, both external and internal. Externally, light and dark, good and bad – internally, health and disease. 'Without dark we would not know the light. Without death we would not know we were alive. Without imperfection we would not know perfection' (Rowe, 1893, p. 101).

The human race lives with the ambiguities of opposites whether they inhabit the two Third World areas where the survival of war and poverty is top of the agenda, or the rich western third of the globe. Night and day, love and hate, anger and harmony, peace and war march side by side in every human being, in every community and on every continent. A person's emotional and spiritual strength will depend on such external contrasts and internal resources. This will determine how individuals live their lives.

The World and How it Affects the Clergy

This was pertinent to this research. It has already been noted that the historical and sociological changes have had a profound effect on the Church of England. This, coupled with the ordination of women to the priesthood and the consequent rift this caused, as well as the ongoing debate about gay clergy, has appeared to inflict a near fatal wound upon the institution. No longer is the Church of England seen in good standing in the country. No longer are the clergy respected for their erudition. No longer are the majority of people drawn to the dispensers of salvific mystery. As many of the clergy have stated, 'I am an irrelevance and so is the Church.'

Many who work for large business and commercial organisations experience stress and burnout, or experience the trauma of redundancy. The feeling of being useless and of no importance operates at every level of society.

It may be that clergy are immune from all of this. They are seldom, if ever, made redundant, and certainly not if they have the freehold of their parish. They are only removed from the office through 'conduct unbecoming the life and work of a clerk in holy orders and neglect of duty' (Leeder, 1997, p. 403). They have a lot of responsibility under the bishop. In practice, the incumbent exercises accountability without much reference to the hierarchy at all. They are, as has already been stated, iconic figures for their congregations. The uniform they wear adds cohesion to their role and status, providing them with a mask behind which to hide. So why is it that so many of the clergy admit to being stressed and finding it hard to cope?

Surely much of the answer to this has to do with the clergy's sense of irrelevance in the culture in which they live. It is as though on the one hand the work they do proclaims the Gospel message they profoundly believe in. On the other hand, no one else appears to do so. That, for many clergy, feels like crying in the wind – all the time swimming against the tide. Those who have a well-integrated identity are more able to find the opposing forces exciting and challenging. Those with a fragile sense of self appear unable to do that. They need the affirmation of the hierarchy, the congregation and those around, to affirm their indistinct self-image. When this is not forthcoming, their belief system does not appear robust enough to defend against fragmentation.

The Paradox of the Christian Faith

In many ways the Christian faith is paradoxical. The clergy have learned that the Christian message is about the cross as well as the resurrection, about dying to self as well as receiving new life in Christ Jesus, and about striving as well as coming to him for rest.

The Gospel has never been a soft option. The first disciples endured martyrdom in many gruesome forms. They were not promised a peaceful and easy existence in this life, nor are present-day leaders. There has been no physical persecution of Christians in this country for many centuries (though this has consistently

157

occurred in other countries across the world, in the present as well as the past).

Clergy have little financial remuneration but they do have certain work advantages. By and large their job is secure and they usually live in a house larger than others in the parish and larger than they would be able to afford if in secular employment. After serving their curacies they are put in charge of a parish and so are able to exercise total responsibility for the church's work in that area.

The Emotional and Spiritual Health of the Clergy

This last area to be explored in the research examined the emotional and spiritual life of the clergy. Questions to do with what being a priest meant to them, the stress they suffered, times of loss of faith or doubts, how they expressed anger – were all explored. The clergy shared the worst time and the best time they had experienced in their ministry, as well as their feelings about the amount of support they did or did not receive from the hierarchy. They were asked if they had ever felt like giving up.

By the time this area of the interview was reached the clergy were sharing openly and honestly. Many of them felt this was the crux of ministry – whether they were able to cope with the daily demands of the work, the intrusiveness into their private lives and the effect it had on their close family and friends. The internal reaction to the external pressures had a direct effect on their emotional and spiritual health. It was difficult to estimate whether, if they were spiritually strong, they were more emotionally stable or whether, if they were emotionally stable their spiritual life remained intact.

The question was divided into two parts – emotional and spiritual – though this was an artificial division, for each had a direct bearing on the other.

Emotional Strength

Figure 10 shows the different categories that were delineated to express the clergy's emotional strength.

The categories generated were derived from the implicit communications from the material collected and my own perceptions of the respondents' emotional health. The limitation of such categorisation was that it depended on how the clergy presented themselves on the day of the interview. This was largely determined by the events of the days before, their immediate relationships and their physical wellbeing.

This did however allow for these themes to emerge from the data.

The emotional strength of the clergy interviewed

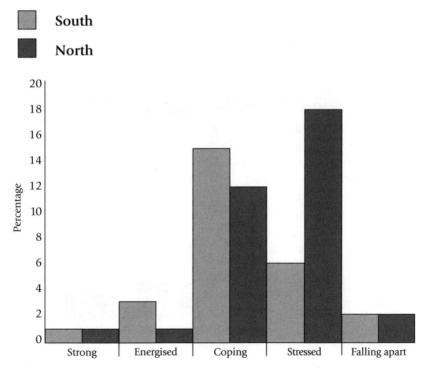

Figure 10

Emotional Strength and the Ageing Process

Figure 11 looks at the breakdown of the different ages into each category. It is interesting to note that none of the younger clergy were experiencing a sense of falling apart. Only within the middle-aged bracket did clergy experience the full range of emotions. This group would be dealing with adolescent children and ageing parents; disenchantment with their career prospects; spouses (mainly wives) starting new careers, as well as the inner emotional turmoil that these events raise.

The emotional strength of different age groups that were interviewed

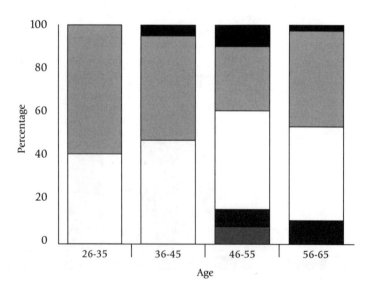

Figure 11

The over 55s were beginning to think about the last job they would do. Several expressed anger that they had not been considered for preferment. They felt their gifts had not been recognised and that many clergy occupying hierarchical posts were less gifted than they felt they were. There was also the dilemma at that stage of life as to when to look for work in another parish. If they started a new work at 50, some felt they would then spend too long in one place before they retired. If they delayed looking for a parish until their late 50s they knew that fewer parishes would be interested. Most parishes are looking for an incumbent in their early 40s, married with children. This is very stressful for older clergy, who can easily reach retirement feeling disillusioned and passed over.

Integration and Individuation

These are different words used to describe the person who appears to manage life and all its vicissitudes in a responsible and mature way.

Many of the clergy appeared to place enormous significance on the support they gained from their spouse, the hierarchy or the parish. The state of their emotional health seemed to rest within 'objects' outside themselves. However, when the Church ordained women priests, this was experienced as an attack. Equally, if the parish or hierarchy did not affirm and value them it seemed they were therefore rejecting and abandoning them, or the parish was turning its back on them. For those with an unclearly defined identity, this may have had a direct result on the emotional integration or otherwise of the clergy.

Rayburn, Richmond and Rogers (1986), in their studies on stress amongst religious leaders, found that they experienced a lower overall occupational stress and personal strain than the rest of the population. Stress is a recognised problem amongst those within the caring professions. Clergy stress occurs because of 'work overload, (too many meetings to the detriment of pastoral work, time pressures); role conflicts (balancing family and work priorities, conflicts between planned and crisis work, church conservation); role ambiguity . . . .; dealing with grief and people in need . . . .; relationships with parishioners and parish (unrealistic demands . . .); and self pressures (inability to say no, not appreciating one's own limitations, difficulties in delegating)' (Francis and Jones, 1996, p. 134).

During the interviewing, it appeared that most of the clergy felt they suffered from emotional stress. How much did that preclude them from functioning at an appropriate level? How much was it a sign that they had not yet reached a state of integration? If clergy appeared to lack integration and individuation, were there then clear pointers to highlight an adequate response by the Church to their psychological needs? This became clearer as each category was explored, investigating their emotional strength.

Strong

This category denoted a strong integrated ego with all the psychological signs that integration and individuation had occurred. Only two male priests came within this category. Both described themselves as Modern Catholics.

1. Stable Family Life

These priests came from Church backgrounds and attended day schools, and described their childhood as happy. One saw his priesthood as representative, whilst the other believed he was more of a pastor. Though he also saw himself as a representative priest, he did not want to 'get in the way of people seeing God'. He was therefore not representing God, but enabling others to find him. Interestingly, both were only children from working class families.

One priest lived very near some cousins, so was brought up in an extended family. The other said he was not academically gifted as 'it was not until Secondary School that they realised I was as blind as a bat'. His father contracted tuberculosis and was very ill for several years. That was a difficult time: 'Father and I didn't speak for a long time. I'm sure it was just a male territorial thing. When I left home we became very good friends. We weren't a threat to each other any more.'

2. Supportive Partners

One priest was married with children. Though his wife had her own profession, she still saw it as her role to support him and to keep him 'on the rails'.

The other was in a stable homosexual relationship of 14 years. His partner worked outside the Church and was not permanently resident in the parish. He described the relationship as 'deeply supportive and helpful'. He described coming to his parish seven years before as a crucifixion. 'The last Vicar had left because of it. I decided the gay issue would have to come out. It was in the national papers. We have never kept it secret, but it became a resurrection. We were seen as a couple, there was no hiding, only freedom.' He said that there was also a very good editorial in a local paper about his previous ministry. This priest said he had always been able to receive support from the hierarchy.

3. The Joy of Priesthood

This priest said, 'I enjoy every minute of being a priest. When I wake up I want to get on with priesting. It invades every part of my life, whether I'm in the pub or not.' He appeared to be saying that he was unable to withdraw from being a priest. It gave meaning to his life, and a sense of identity. Though the 'invasion' implies intrusiveness, this priest welcomed rather than rejected such a plight. He said that he now gets less stressed as he can stand back from things and is more laid back: 'Each Lent I have a sorting out time when I go on retreat.' The only stress he felt was because he was in his 50s and not his 30s and so had less adrenaline flowing. Though the parish could be stressful, he said, 'I don't get deep stress. I never ask why am I here and what am I doing? I never want to give up and open up a teashop.' He said that he was not an angry person but seemed to 'explode every five years and that lasts ten seconds'. He explained that people knew when he was annoyed.

The married clergyman said, 'I never thought of being anything else but a priest. I feel very fulfilled and happy.' At the time of interview, he was thinking about moving and had been shortlisted for a job, but he was not overconcerned if nothing turned up in the immediate future.

4. Dealing with Conflict

He said, 'I've not suffered from stress, though I nearly did this year.' He was chairing a lay committee on which they spent two years planning for a large diocesan occasion. His colleagues in the parish released him from preaching for three months to allow it to be more manageable. He said that 'two thirds of the diocesan clergy did not support the event or encourage their parishes to support it'. He believed clergy have developed a 'bunker mentality and do not want to know of anything going on outside their own churches and parishes'. He said, 'Lay leaders are often hampered by less than supportive clergy. I believe so much of what happens depends on the clergy being on board. If they're not, the laity lose heart. I do believe the freehold should go and that clergy should have renewable contracts of five or seven years.' He said he was a placid man who did not often show anger. 'If I get angry then I talk it out. I don't rant and rave. I bounce things off my wife. My worst time was six months before I was ordained. I had got through my finals and just felt totally dry. I did not know which way to go. I'd sailed through the course up to that time so it was very hard. Another difficult time was when I was in a very tough parish. The work took up a lot of my time when the children were small and my wife needed me and we didn't have much money.' When talking about support from the hierarchy, he said he did not know what the clergy were really looking for: 'We can pick up the phone and ask to see someone at any time.'

Discussion

Both these clergy had experienced pressurised times for different reasons. However, they had faced the challenge and had never doubted the rightness of their call to ordained ministry. Not only that, they had supportive partners who were equally fulfilled in their own chosen careers. There was no competition about whose job came first, though when and if the married priest was offered a job some distance away, his wife would have to relocate her work. The other interesting fact that came out of the data was that neither clergy talked of being 'passed over'. They were content with where they were. Though the married priest was looking for a job within the hierarchy, he said, 'If that doesn't happen I am happy to remain a parish priest, for that was what I was ordained for.'

Energised

A definition of energy: 'a capacity for action . . . effective power . . . the capacity for doing work and overcoming resistance' (*The Collins Pocket Dictionary*, 1981). Five of the clergy from the sample came under this category. They exhibited many of the attributes of the two clergy in the previous category.

However, these priests' backgrounds, life experiences and relationship status were very varied. One was divorced, one single, two married with children and the female priest was married without children. Three of the men were not brought up in Christian homes, whereas the female priest's father was a Vicar and the other male priest's parents went to church. Two of the clergy were sent to boarding school and one male priest described his childhood as very lonely because his parents worked hard all the time. This clergyman had also experienced the loss of an elder brother who died of drowning when he was only 3 years old. A couple of them had experienced what they described as 'breakdowns' in the early part of their ministry.

Despite this there was an energy and enthusiasm about these clergy. They enjoyed their work in spite of all the frustrations. Stress for them was part of the job, and not a debilitating symptom that prevented them from functioning. They appeared to be well integrated. Though the female priest controlled her life in every detail, she was aware of why she needed to do that. The counselling course she had attended had given her some insight into how she functioned. Her self-awareness made her avoid any situation that repeated her mother's verbal assaults.

1. Managing Stress

One of these priests was an open Evangelical and said, 'I don't like the word "priest". I'm here to minister, lead and serve the people of God.' He went on to say that he had never suffered from stress. 'When I started in ministry I got very tired. I then used to have a half-hour sleep in the afternoon. Now I just go to bed very tired at night.'

He said that in the early years of ministry he got depressed because he was so tired. He found playing clergy cricket helped him. He said he never shouted when he became angry, but his feelings were heard in his voice. One of his worst experiences was when two leaders in his church had an affair. The other was when he and his family moved to their present parish. 'I had not been prepared for the sense of bereavement I felt. I had been at that parish for 15 years and had prayed with people and seen them grow up. It was a real sense of loss and I wasn't ready for it.' He had never found it difficult to phone up an archdeacon or bishop if he needed help.

2. Confronting Conflict

The female priest said, 'I have very little tolerance of difficult feelings and I want to do something about it early on. I've never suffered from stress as I confront it straight away. I *never* get worn out. I'm not a weak person and I will not allow myself to be bullied.' The only time she admitted to feeling weak was when she got ill. She felt she ought to accept it but didn't. She said, 'I don't express anger, as I am too rational. As anger in my family was expressed violently, my mother shouted and screamed, I make sure I don't do that but I do answer back. I give as good as I get. People expect women to be gentle.' Her worst time had been in her curacy, when her vicar asked her to leave. 'I told him I would take him to an Industrial Tribunal. Instead, I went to the bishop. When I eventually moved, the vicar was on the verge of a nervous breakdown.'

There was a quiet ruthlessness about this lady. To survive she employed logic and reason to everything. The defences she had built around her felt inviolate. However, if any of them crumbled there did not appear to be much to take their place. She had a very small parish, plus an extra-parochial post. She was happy and self-sufficient with no visible crack to be seen. At the end of the interview the unspoken questions which hovered in the air were, 'What will happen if all of this crumbles?' and 'How will you cope?'

3. Integration of Vulnerability

One priest seemed far more open to his own vulnerability. He said, 'I get self-regard from the audience who listens to me. Friendships feed me. Though I have a love-hate relationship with the parish, weddings, funerals and baptisms all feed me. I am a natural pessimist but I seem to have a buoyancy now. I find the hierarchy is more supportive and I have a "senior" friend to talk to and to confess to. Ministerial education is very helpful.' He said that he did get angry, but he introverted it. 'I get my aggression out listening to aggressive symphonies. The hardest time has been when we moved to our last parish and seeing the bright ideas I had wouldn't work and they were rejected. I find the worst thing is being a new boy in the place.'

This priest had 'fallen in love' with a woman in the last parish. 'Though it was a very difficult time and I hurt a lot of people, I learned a lot about redemption. Also, I used to feel I couldn't complete the task as I hadn't any energy but not now. I do what I can.'

Again, this priest had travelled a long way. Unlike the female priest, he had used his times of brokenness for integration. He gained much self-esteem from others but, nevertheless, had a much clearer self-image than previously.

4. From Brokenness to Individuation

A single priest who lived in a warm, comfortable home, said, 'Being a priest is something which I have become and I can't see myself outside this role.' As a young man he had sustained a severe breakdown. 'I was the blue-eyed boy in the diocese. They got me to go on an exchange. I lasted six weeks there. It was horrendous. When I got home the diocese gave me six months to get myself back together. They then offered me a parish which would have pushed me back into breakdown. My confidence had completely gone so, instead, I went and trained as a teacher and I stayed teaching for 10 years. This rebuilt my confidence and I learned a lot. Before, I had lost all sense of colour. I found it was all to do with a dependency on my parents and my sexuality. I just had a great sense of loneliness. That was the worst time in my ministry and when I came back I was treated like a pariah. I felt there were weak links in the hierarchy where things were not handled properly, and so no support was given.'

Now he feels he copes better with stress. 'I have learned to say "no" if I am getting fraught. I can swear with, and at, friends and my housekeeper. I rarely retaliate in anger. I am pretty controlled.' He described the best time in his ministry as now. He enjoyed all the extra parochial jobs he did and knew who to go to in the diocese if he needed to. Unlike the female priest, whose home was guarded by double five-barred gates, this priest's home exuded warmth and comfort. He had learned how to nurture his inner being as well as being available to others.

5. Serve to Lead

One of the divorced clergymen had been an Army officer. He described priesthood as 'a job like any other, but it works within the idea of servanthood. The motto at Sandhurst was 'Serve to Lead'. I believe that sums up the Christian profession with the emphasis on prizing people, caring for them and working with and for them.' He described how he had a breakdown 10 years ago when his wife left. 'Though others may describe it as a mental breakdown, it was a spiritual thing for me. It was a *reforming* moment in my life as it opened me up much more to God and off-loaded a lot of historic memory, pain and clobber and gave me a sharper focus on God.'

He had three months off work, but it reformed him and it got 'a lot of inner tension' out of him. 'I went to Burrswood for three weeks and then to Hillfield Priory. I had some counselling and spiritual direction, which helped.' At the time his wife thought he 'was barmy'. It was frightening for her.

They had had a very difficult experience during his curacy. 'I had a very bullish vicar who said, "If you can't do the job then get out". My wife was on valium and we had young children. It broke her expectations of a caring Church. I don't think she ever recovered.' He felt the Church hierarchy was very poor at giving support.

This priest came over as a 'man with a mission'. He was a dedicated priest with one aim – God and the job. His broken marriage, and the fact he had never wanted to marry again bore testimony to that. He had been through a lot, and that came across. He was a caring but insightful man, and had arrived at a place that felt manageable for him.

Discussion

The clergy were open about the breakdowns they had suffered. These traumatic experiences had reshaped their lives. They had learned how to manage themselves and their workloads more effectively. Symptoms of stress acted like a barometer to enable them to take responsibility for themselves. They could now say 'no' to unreasonable demands, which gave them the energy they needed for their work.

Coping

The largest numbers of clergy came within the coping and stress categories. As Figure 10 shows, more northern clergy admitted to being stressed than southern clergy. Those within this category admitted to being stressed, but appeared to be able to manage it well enough for their work not to deteriorate.

The following categories were either explicit or implicit in the data collected.

1. Self-induced Stress

One priest said, 'I suffer from stress but it is partly self-induced. It is the irrational guilt that I'm not doing enough. I don't always feel fresh and so give tired sermons and have to cut corners. I would feel stronger if I had more time.'

This priest had a small parish in terms of population, but ministered to three different congregations and three churches. He had never wanted to be ordained but couldn't get away from the call. He found that stress had affected his health. He had high blood pressure and was a diabetic. He got angry at the whole Church system and 'people's totally unrealistic and irrational expectations'. He felt let down: 'If I had been teaching I would be fairly senior now. I feel I should have been a bishop or archdeacon by now.'

He felt that the negatives stemmed from the structure and mechanics of the Church. 'Sometimes I feel a terrible failure and the worst time is when no one bothers with me and just lets me get on with it. It is bad feeling you don't matter or count for very much.' He said, 'I feel clergy are left to get on with it. I would like more encouragement. I would like the bishop to say, "You're doing a good job." I would like appraisals that identify what's good and what is bad. I do have visits from the bishop and archdeacon but it's not enough. They need to face issues and bare souls and work things through with the parishioners. I feel very lonely at times.'

He was near retirement and wondered if he had much more to give. At times he had felt as though he were drowning.

All of this sounded very negative. As he continued to talk, however, he said, 'The happiness far outweighs the unhappiness, because I'm doing the job God wanted me to do so I do feel very fulfilled. I believe being a priest is about the giving the whole of the time. I try to minister the love and compassion of God and make people feel valued and that I'm there for them at any given moment.' He went on to say that he had a good bishop who conducted yearly visitations.

2. Disabling Stress

Another priest said, 'I used to enjoy stress until I became disabled. I used to be a character built for . . . challenges and difficulties, but the illness has lessened my emotional control by 10 to 15 per cent. I have to exercise discipline to keep calm, and any emotional upheaval worsens my condition.' He then went on to describe his daily battle with coping with very basic, everyday elements of living. Sometimes the pain was intense and then he ranted at God and said: 'You only had if for three hours.' He said he had this year learned to accept the immense kindness, help and support from others. 'I have had to rebuild my theology of humanity. I used to be fairly Calvinistic, expecting to be let down by people, but the love and care has been salutary.'

His worst time in ministry was when working abroad amidst great poverty. It was very hard for his wife and children. He said, 'All the ministry has been best, it's been wonderful. Now I have to learn that the Church can grow without me. Our bishop is more concerned than any predecessor, and has been there when needed.'

This priest saw his illness as a 'calling'. He was on a journey, and everything was in terms of him being a follower of Christ and a servant of the living God. Though his pain and frustration were obvious, he was still a man full of ideas for living, though realistic about his approaching death. The whole interview was a very humbling experience.

3. Guilty Stress

A similar theme of guilt emerged with another incumbent. He said, 'I spend my time feeling guilty as I always feel I should be doing something else. If I'm preparing I feel I should be visiting, if visiting, I should be preparing. I can never really relax. Things keep coming at me so I feel I'm either neglecting the parish or not educating the congregation. I do suffer from stress. I find it hard to sleep at times, and will wake up and go downstairs and watch a video. When I get angry I swear, but not publicly. Sometimes I've felt like giving up, especially as people are not coming to church and I feel I'm banging my head against a brick wall. I've felt I've had to prove I can do it in a new job.'

The worst time in ministry was when he was a team vicar. He

had a very bad relationship with the team rector. 'I was scared of him. He once grabbed my arm and left bruises on it. I called in the bishop and archdeacon but we still had to stay there for eight months, and we just did not dare go out of the house.' He did not feel supported by the hierarchy, but by the Rural Dean. He was eventually sent to work in a parish which was 'very restorative and healing, especially to be ministering again. My wife stayed in the house for four months and didn't go to church. It took her a long time to recover.'

He said that his wife helped him relax, and that he had lots of good times. He said, 'The priestly role is caring for people, weeping with those that weep, and rejoicing with those that rejoice. It is the cross and resurrection coming together and that I can't have one without the other.'

4. The Unpredictability of the Job

One priest had been divorced and remarried. He said, 'It is a great privilege to celebrate the sacraments and to have access to people's homes. I come up against all sorts of emotions on a day-to-day basis. I could be doing a child's funeral and then have to go straight off and do a wedding. It does provide a balance, but I do wonder how long we will have access to people's homes before we have to provide identity cards. The unsociable hours and unpredictability of the job are very draining. I do suffer from emotional stress, especially when people are not responding.' He went on to say he can get irritable and withdrawn, and would blow up in a controlled way.

5. Joyful Stress

Several priests expressed the emotional joy and privilege of being a priest. One said, 'I like being the centre of attention. I like to be needed, though some days I do wish not so many people needed me.'

This young, single priest appeared at interview to want to please. He talked of his sexuality as a 'grey area'. He was very young when put in charge of a parish of 9000 people. He felt he would have liked a pat on the back from the hierarchy, 'someone to notice and care'. He found when he was stressed he could not sleep.

6. Bereavement

A female, single priest, said, 'When I get stressed I get spots and I have stomach ache.' She said she goes silent when she gets angry. She found her worst time was leaving her previous parish a few years earlier. 'The loss of friends and the sharp learning curve when I came here. It was also difficult to find people leaving this Church because I'm a woman. It is hard to be hated, but it is everything to preach, celebrate the Eucharist and to visit. It is like breathing.' She said that when she was in training she could phone up the bishop. Now she was managing, no one asked how it was all going.

Another priest said, 'Being a priest for me is my secret love affair with my Creator.' He said it was not a threat to his wife, as he could not love her any more. He said, 'I've suffered from stress. I suffered depression at college, when the girl I thought I was going to marry jilted me. Now if I'm tired and I get irritable I use escape valves – days off, family, going out for a drink and a meal, playing sport.' Fifteen years ago this priest had a blocked carotid artery. He was not off work, but had scans – 'but I've never felt like giving up'.

7. Burnout

Another clergyman said, 'I got very, very burnt out in a demanding parish. I got depressed and ran out of steam.' It was a very difficult parish where the previous vicar had survived only six weeks and then had a heart attack. It had five worship centres and 21 Parochial Church Council meetings a year. He said, 'I was radically disjointed.'

8. Intrusion from the Past

Another priest was told a few days before he was instituted that the previous vicar had been sacked. 'He only lives a couple of miles down the road. He kept coming into the parish every day, meeting with one of the wardens and undermining all I was trying to do. When I went and visited a bereaved family, I found he'd been there before me and had arranged to do the service. He still had the keys to the rectory and he'd come and wait for the post-man for his letters. I felt like giving up several times as the Church people gave me hell.' This priest felt unsupported by the hierarchy.

He still felt it was a privilege to be ordained, though he did not have a high view of the priesthood, believing it is like any other job. The stressful time he went through caused him loss of sleep.

9. Crucifixion

For one of the clergy, being a priest is about entering into his own pain and other people's, and into the sacrifice of Christ. 'It is not an ego trip. I suffer from stress imposed by other people's expectations. I never can meet them but I have a sense of not being a private person. The office is an awesome one as it is a burden being the representative figure of the divine, of God.'

Another felt that being a priest can be a crucifixion when rejected by the community. 'My children have been tormented because I am the vicar. I have suffered from anger and frustration from the hierarchy because when I needed support it didn't happen. When I was off for five months with a bad back, the bishop came to see me once. He said he'd come back but he didn't. When I phoned about an incident my wife suffered, no one returned the call so I felt angry, as I would care much more for my own people in the parish who are not churchgoers.'

He said that his ordination was the best time. 'I was naïve and full of hope and expectations, beginning a new venture with God.'

A female priest said, 'I've never suffered from stress, though I had an allergy after doing a funeral of a soldier who had been in Ireland. It got reported in the paper that I had condemned the IRA. I then got obscene letters. I went to the doctor who said I was depressed. I couldn't stop sleeping. But being a priest is my life. That's why it is hard to have days off.'

Discussion

Most of the clergy in this category said they suffered from stress most of the time. Often it manifested itself physically. A 65-year-old priest said, 'I am conscious of being tired all the time and I suffer from a sense of disease and unhappiness.' He had not felt supported by his bishop and had, at times, felt misunderstood.

Several of these priests said they'd thought of giving up. One at least had embarked upon another career after being ordained, because of a mental breakdown and not being able to cope with the stresses of parochial life. Stress appeared to be activated by poor relationships with colleagues; other people's expectations; physical illness; the close proximity of a previous vicar; being young and at the beginning of ministry; being near retirement, and feeling tired and passed over for preferment; too large a parish; too complex a parish; and the breakdown of a marital relationship.

It has already been stated that the late 50s is a very difficult stage for clergy. One priest had been in his parish for over seven years. Now at 59 years old there was no prospect of another parish, let alone preferment. He had 'rejected' the lifestyle of his parents for what they felt 'was an alien profession'. At the end of his priestly ministry this priest was expressing a feeling of being rejected by his 'adoptive' parents – that was the Church.

In spite of all this, the clergy have echoed each other in stating the importance of their ministry to them. They have used superlatives to describe what it means to them to be a priest. Because of this, the joy appears to have outweighed the stress. This had enabled them to cope well enough in their situations – often feeling a sense of disintegration, but with enough sense of identity to continue. At a very basic level they enjoyed their work and could not imagine themselves doing any other.

Stressed

The largest number of those in this category came from the northern diocese – in fact twice as many as from the south. The majority of southern clergy who admitted to being stressed nevertheless often felt able to cope with their work. It is within this group of clergy from both north and south that there were more who were unable to cope. The largest number of clergy feeling stressed and not coping very well came within the 36 to 45 age bracket. The 56 to 65 age group also experienced a commensurate amount of stress. It has already been noted that the younger group were often in their first incumbencies whilst the older group were at the end of their working life.

1. Physical Illness

One incumbent felt 'incredibly privileged to be a priest. Basically, congregations love their priest and will do anything for them. I do feel very supported and cared for.' In spite of this he continued by saying, 'I have suffered from irritable bowel syndrome for 10 to 15 years. My blood pressure is also being controlled. I do get depressed, though not clinically depressed, and it doesn't usually last long, but I have felt I could at times get in my car and just drive off. I do flare up when angry and I take it out on the children and I do react in a totally disproportionate manner.'

His worst time in ministry was his first incumbency. The previous priest had had an affair with a church member. At that time he 'found it very hard coming back from holiday and driving back into the parish'.

2. Mental Illness

One priest said, 'I have had depression on and off for as long as I can remember. Being a priest is about guilt. My inadequacy in not getting things done. I see other priests doing things so much better than I can do them that I feel very ineffective. My father and gran both had psychiatric help, and my father suffers from panic attacks. If I feel depressed I tidy things up. I don't sleep. I used to wonder if I had the psychological stamina to be a priest.'

This very young single priest said, 'I have thought about running away but I have a ministerial consultant so have someone to talk to. At least as a priest I have a place in the community and I feel needed. I'm known and recognised in the market place.'

Another priest said, 'I feel I had a breakdown because my wife couldn't cope with me raising my voice or being angry. I had a curate who had three brilliant ideas before breakfast every day and a mother in a local nursing home. At the same time, my wife suffered from repetitive strain injury so I had to do everything. I had to drive her to work and do everything in the house. It was a nightmare. I had ten weeks off work and went away and had a period of brokenness. I wept in church and prayed and things gradually came together. During that time I had felt suicidal and that people would be better off without me. I did not feel I could go to the archdeacon or the bishop, as I felt so ashamed. I felt like giving up.'

Another priest said, 'I was off sick for six months. Two church councils waged a hate campaign against me in my last parish, and treated me as though I didn't exist. I kept wanting to burst into tears and could not put one foot in front of the other emotionally. But being a priest is something much bigger. As Julian of Norwich said, "All shall be well, all shall be well, all manner of things shall be well." I have come to terms with the isolation and loneliness. It is part of the human condition.' This priest had been married and divorced twice.

3. Marriage Break-up

A 63-year-old priest said, 'The worst time was when my first marriage broke up. I did not want it to, as I believed in my marriage vows. I felt I had let the ideals down and been betrayed as a priest. I would not want to be ordained now. I get stressed because of what happens in our communities. I have a contempt for injustice.'

Describing his marriage break-up this priest said he felt the hierarchy were useless. 'When my first wife left with the children I was in terrible darkness. I would cry every day for hours. I would come in from the parish and cook tea and just cry and cry.'

4. Burn-out

One priest said, 'I don't know what it means to be a priest. I don't really feel like a priest. In my last job I got completely exhausted and I left the job to escape. I was close to tears most of the time. Now I'm experiencing a loss of faith, so I'm coping by talking and exploring with friends and my wife. What is difficult is that I can't just go off and have a crisis of faith. Being a priest is my work, life, home and everything. If I lose faith and leave, then it affects my wife and children and I can't do that to them.'

He went on to say that people find his anger difficult to handle, though it rarely comes out and he is pretty controlled. Because he is a large person his anger can be terrifying and would discredit the Church. He said, 'The worst time has been the last ten years. I haven't enjoyed this job though I like the nice house and it has paid for the children's education, but I find the people's smugness and middle-classness irritating.' Because he had never been offered any preferment he felt angry and depressed.

5. Family Pressures

A young priest said, 'The worst time was when my wife had a nervous breakdown two years ago. It was triggered by stress in work and concern for the children and me. She had never really recovered from postnatal depression. It had been hard for her to move from our previous parish, which was only eight miles away. Also, people were not very welcoming here. I just had to get her away. Her parents looked after the children.' This priest said he had had good written support from the bishop, a visit from the Rural Dean, some money for a holiday but *no* visit from the archdeacon or bishop. He felt very hurt by that.

6. Ordination of Women

Two of the women in this category have experienced anger over the ordination of women. One said, 'I did not get enough support. I asked God why he didn't like women.' Another female priest found it very hard, in a cathedral service, to observe only male priests round the altar. She said, 'I've had a rocky year. I've had a lot of opposition and I've had shingles, which is a sign of stress. I have lost my faith in the Church but I can take my anger out on my piano, or by throwing books. I feel it is crazy being expected to run three parishes. I wonder if I'm in the right place. I felt very alone when my husband died, it was a real Gethsemane, but being a priest is what I'm best suited to do, so in spite of everything I do have a deep-down contentment.'

One female priest experienced a lot of stress over the last two years because the team rector has a deteriorating illness. She continued: 'Also, I have problems working with one of the team vicars. There is a real clash of personality. I alerted the bishop and the Rural Dean but nothing was done. I am now menopausal and have experienced acute stress. I don't believe the work patterns imposed are really helpful for women with children. They are all right for men. They can attend early services but I can't as I have children to get off to school. I feel the hierarchy have been abysmal. My husband is a great support and does everything in the house.'

Another woman wonders, 'Why has God asked me to do so much that is demanding? When I am totally given to God I just get absolutely drained and exhausted.' For her, being a priest was 'saying "yes" to God'.

Discussion

Several people in this category expressed disappointment in their bishops. They felt unsupported when they needed help. In some instances they experienced lack of support in looking for jobs when they had had to leave their present posts.

They feel that bishops should spend more time going round parishes and less time on high-profile conferences. They believe the work of a bishop is to be pastor to the priests in the parishes.

Those whose marriages had broken down were disappointed in what they experienced as lack of care from their bishops. This was equally true for those clergy whose wives had been sick.

These clergy appeared, at times, very near the edge. However, at the time of the interview they were still managing their jobs and functioning at an appropriate level. It was clear, though, that their disease was only just below the surface.

Falling Apart

Four clergy admitted to feeling fragmented – two from the north and two from the south. Two of these, one from each diocese, had recently experienced their wives leaving them. The other two (again, one from each diocese), were suffering depression, one because he had moved from his previous parish due to the arrival of a woman priest, and he did not believe women should be ordained priest. This priest had been placed in a very deprived area where there was a lot of violence. The other had been in hospital after falling over an animal and suffering a haematoma. All four of these clergy, for different reasons, were barely coping with life. They had been off work for weeks, were suffering from depression, and appeared anxious and desperate.

Listening to them a sense of hopelessness and darkness was frequently expressed. At the time of the interview there appeared no escape from these intolerable feelings.

1. Hopelessness

One priest said, 'I feel I'm going back into a chrysalis. I'm not sure whether I'm going to die or emerge again as a butterfly. I feel I'm at the end of the cycle of renewal and death. Christ has taught me the patience of suffering, but I'm not looking for resurrection.' As he talked he expressed his deep concern for the Church of England. He felt his own church would close and that the Church was deeply exhausted. He said: 'I have no more guts in me to cope with death and resurrection. I feel I am dying now.' He said he was suffering a lot of stress and that's why he was on medication. He had been having panic attacks. 'I had a sabbatical planned but my wife did not want me to go. I thought the sabbatical would renew me in my job but it was all too difficult – lots of conflict about who would pay. I now just want time to read. I used to express my anger with a cricket bat, now I cut the grass.' When asked what had been the worst time in his ministry he said, 'Now! There is no hope here. I want to give up. People don't want to hear my sermons.' He was a very deeply depressed man!

2. Dark Night of the Soul

Another priest disclosed how, leaving his last parish because of the arrival of a female priest, he went through a dark night of the soul. 'The stress was real and palpable. It took a long time to move as I had many interviews and didn't get a job. My arm was twisted to accept this job. My father was a depressive. I have never had depression before so it's been very frightening. I have been off for four months with shingles, 'flu and depression. Our physical location on this housing estate is very bad. We suffer a lot of vandalism and sheer wanton hooliganism. I find the confrontation and violence very hard and demoralising. I haven't been trained to deal with people who urinate against the back door!' He felt the hierarchy had been very good during his illness.

3. Breakdown

The two remaining clergy in this group were experiencing breakdown because their wives had left them some months prior to the interview. One said, 'It's the function of the priesthood that gets in the way of family life. I spent very little time with the family when the children were small. With my wife working the last few years, and commuting to other parts of the country, we have spent very little time together. There used to be five ordained members of staff here before I came. One left, one had a breakdown. The curate left, and the other non-stipendiary woman priest caused all the problems, and eventually had to be asked to leave.'

He felt that the irritation of the work was the reason why his wife had left. He believed that his family was very proud that he was a priest but said, 'My wife couldn't cope with carrying my burdens as well as her own. I've decided I'm leaving the parochial ministry, as I can't take it any more. I want to do something totally different.'

The other priest said, 'The last two months since my wife left have been a blank. I've had a breakdown though I have not been hospitalised, but I couldn't manage the business of living. I once went out and bought 20lbs of Cumberland sausages. I haven't smoked for 13 years but since my wife left I chain-smoke. This has been the worst time in my ministry. I felt as though I had died. I'm just beginning to come out of it and I'm just beginning to see what the future holds. The Church hierarchy have been very good.' He said, 'Being a priest is very deep. It is about who and what I am. I both love and hate it but it is a passionate way of life.'

Discussion

All four of these clergy were, at interview, experiencing a sense of deep fragmentation. They were not working and in different ways were trying to find a way back to life. Themes of death and the cross were expressed alongside feelings of desperation and loss of faith. Far from feeling integrated, these clergy were disintegrated. They were, indeed, 'cracked pots' with a sense they may never get the pieces back together again.

It was very clear that the emotional strength/weakness and internal integration had a direct bearing on how the clergy coped with the pressures from the community and the rest of their lives. These findings provided validity for the hypotheses suggested.

This category was not just exploring the emotional strengths of these clergy but also their spiritual strengths. In looking at the totality of the results of the interviews of the sample clergy, those who were experiencing the greater sense of dis-ease also found their faith letting them down. For many, the cry was 'Where is God in all of this?' Several expressed their disbelief that there was a God who cared at all. It was a sadness to witness those who so much needed to feel the holding love of the God they had sacrificed everything for, feel instead that he appeared to be non-existent.

Spiritual Health

'Religion concerns itself with the meaning and value of life . . . with the thirst for freedom and grace, with the need for a love that is removed from the unbearable uncertainties of earthly life . . . religious harmony can lift the life of man, . . . which can strengthen the heart, and . . . can elevate the value of existence' (Meissner, 1984, p. 99).

An Unproven Faith

The Christian faith, a belief in God the Father, the Son and the Holy Spirit, renders the clerical profession distinct from any secular job. In business and commerce a product is produced and sold. The success or not of the enterprise will depend on the product made.

The Christian faith is about just that – faith. It cannot be tested and tried under laboratory conditions, or taken out of wrapping paper and passed around for expert verification. 'Faith is being sure of what we hope for and certain of what we do not see' (Hebrews 11:1).

Though the clergy have the Holy Scriptures as a guide, and the life of Jesus as God revealed in human flesh, there is still nothing for them to grasp hold of. The testimonies of thousands down through the millennia – that there is a God and that he is alive and active in his world now, brings comfort and strengthens hope. Clergy, however, are right in the firing line. When pressures come from within and without, their faith in God may well be put under severe strain.

Because they constantly have to propound a faith in the unseeable, it is of vital importance to them that they believe what they say. If not, then they are living a lie and they are working at a job that has no heart to it. They may be emotionally worn out. If they are spiritually dead as well then their very existence as a priest is open to question. Even more poignantly, if there is no God then the Church has no viability either. The cracks in the pot would then, indeed, split it wide open.

Figure 12 *(see overleaf)* shows the breakdown into different categories of spiritual health.

The spiritual health of the clergy interviewed

 South

North

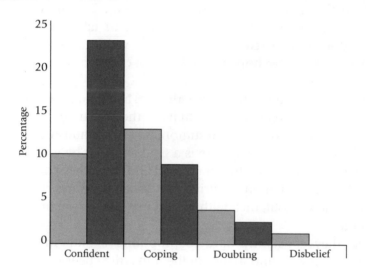

Figure 12

These categories were all derived from my own observations and examining the interviews recorded.

It is interesting to note that though more northern clergy were stressed, yet more northern clergy were confident about their faith. This correlated with the fact that in the north the Church and clergy were not seen as an irrelevance, as they were in the south. Though no more people go to church than in the rest of the country, the Church was still seen as part of the community along with the school and the pub.

The spriritual health of different age groups that were interviewed

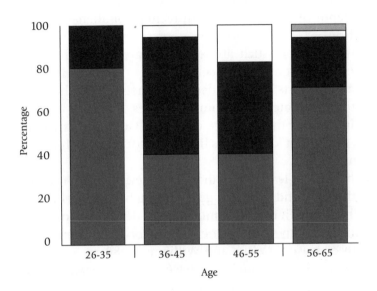

Figure 13

It was noticeable from Figure 13 that for the young clergy faith remained strong. As clergy became older, so doubts increased until, within the upper age group, there were a few who had lost their faith.

The Dark Night of the Soul

This phrase was first coined by the Spanish mystic, John of the Cross (1542-1591) and used subsequently throughout Christendom to denote a depth of spiritual unknowing. 'It describes the work of God upon the soul – not through joy and light but through sorrow and darkness. The concept of the "dark night" has become an integral part of understanding the spiritual journey' (Foster and Smith, 1993, p. 41). It describes the sense of despair and desolation of the believer as they seek God in the blackness. The Christian's sense of sin and unworthiness, added to this barrier that seemed impenetrable, was felt to be between them and their God. The depth of dis-ease results in feelings of alienation and fragmentation.

Those who write of such an experience are those who have spent the most effort and time seeking God in solitude. It is the hermits, the introverts, probing deep into themselves who find, as they try to penetrate the fathomless wastes, that they need to purify their souls in the presence of a holy God. The extrovert, who is out and about 'doing', has little time for and much fear of such darkness.

As will be seen, at least two of those interviewed in this research had been through, and were still going through, these feelings of despair. What brings it on? How much is this despair to do with a loss of faith? For many years 'the debate has too often been about one of faith or reason' (Watts and Williams, 1988, p. 53). With fewer people attending church and fewer coming forward to be ordained, parochial clergy wonder what their life is all about. One clergyman in the southern diocese said, 'The Church is irrelevant and I am an irrelevance to the community here.' Though 'a process of personal transformation is necessarily involved in discovering God' (Watts and Williams, 1988, p. 55), yet there is nothing more likely to bring defeat than the apathy that greets the clergy's best proclamatory efforts Sunday by Sunday. However deep their own convictions, clergy struggle if the laity are not seen to share their enthusiasms – and the laity are much more fickle than they used to be.

How much of this experience is to do with personality, background, and mental or physical disease? Is the dark night of the soul linked to endogenous depression? Can it be tested for during a Selection Conference? Can it be prevented and what does it have to say about the psychological needs of the clergy? The categories describing spiritual health were derived from material collected from the clergy.

Confident

This category highlighted those clergy who, whatever their life experience, appeared to have a belief that God is and that he enjoys a relationship with them.

1. Healthy Doubts

One clergyman said, 'I've never lost my faith but I do have doubts. Then God calls me back to my senses. I've never gone under, as I talk about my doubts to my wife and immerse myself harder in work. If I'm getting on with God's work then that gets it OK again. I have said to God, "Where are you? Is this all a total sham? Have I wasted 30 years of my life? Where are all the converts?" Though I feel I should have been a bishop or archdeacon by now, I can shout at God about any perceived unfairness. I believe God can take it. He's broad-shouldered enough and can put up with my ravings.'

This clergyman's relationship with God seemed personal and intimate. He was able to tell him how he felt and expected God to listen.

2. Questioning Faith

The priest who has retired because of a deteriorating disease, said, 'I have a very open relationship with God. On the day of judgement I will say to him, "The questions you've got lined up for me are only exceeded by the questions I've got lined up for you." I'm not subservient to God. I have a sense of humour; very important. I have never lost faith in God. I may not like him, but I could never deny him.' He said that he saw his priestly ministry as being involved in suffering. 'I have to teach people how to die.'

3. An Isolating Faith

One priest quoted Julian of Norwich (1343-1413) when he said, 'All shall be well, all shall be well, all manner of things shall be well.' I have come to terms with isolation and loneliness. When I'm overwhelmed I'm in the hands of God. I have experienced darkness and had a changing understanding of God. It's felt like going through a crucible, a sort of melting pot. My faith came out deeper. I do have doubts but I can go into church to rant and rave, and I lock the church door.'

This clergyman had been divorced twice and doesn't see the children. He had in many ways, experienced the *dark night of the soul*.

4. A Submitting Faith

A female priest said, 'I have finally submitted to God. My relationship with God has strengthened and deepened. I'm exploring differing ways of seeing and encountering God. I did have a loss of faith when my husband died. I have had doubts too about God's presence. It's as though he has flitted off to look after someone else but it's always the same God.'

One priest has never felt like giving up and said: 'I've never experienced a loss of faith but I do question aspects of faith, like, "Do we live on after death?" I've never felt like giving up.' This priest had also experienced loss. His first wife went off with someone from the church.

5. A Relational Faith

A clergyman described his faith 'as Jesus pitching his tent among us.' He said, 'I've shouted at God about why he's so stupid. Once in Bangladesh I really shouted at him, as I didn't have any money, then a large cheque arrived. I do have lots of doubts, though I have never lost my faith. I do wonder what happens when we die – if the light goes out.'

Another said, 'I've never lost faith except when praying for someone's healing and they aren't, but I've never lost faith in the love of God or atoning sacrifice of Jesus. But does God heal today? My mother-in-law is in appalling health and we are praying for her healing.' He struggled with the prayers God did not answer.

6. A Repentant Faith

A priest said, 'Being a priest is my secret love affair with my Creator. When I've mislaid my faith temporarily, or the mirror has become blurred, the answer for me lies in repentance and getting on doing something. I've never been able to deny my call and my vocation or to talk it away. I've never experienced a loss of faith. I've sometimes thought, "there is no God", but that is academic rather than an existential angst. I say, "If God has moved away, guess who is moved."'

This man had experienced illness and the pain of being jilted.

7. A Servant Faith

The open Evangelical priest had a simple rule. 'Prayer is the way I talk to God, and the Bible is the way God speaks to me. I've never lost my faith and I've never lost sight of being a servant of Christ. My faith has grown and developed. Every moment I have of testing and disappointment I bring to God. I think of God in terms of fatherhood and friendship, but I try to get the balance that he is also King of kings and Lord of lords.'

Discussion

There is a real divergence between religion and psychoanalysis and it is seen in the above and succeeding interviews. 'The religious view of man is specifically supernatural; it envisions man as related to a divine Creator and specifically ordained by that Creator with an idealised and supernaturalised existence. This aspect of the religious perspective has no corollary in the psychoanalytical approach' (Meissner, 1984, p. 216). Meissner goes on to say that a person's religious belief system is either accepted or not.

These clergy were describing their experience and understanding of faith and their own relationship with God. It was their statement and so there were no grounds for accepting it or rejecting it. It was. That had to be enough.

None of these clergy had experienced a loss of faith. They shouted and argued with God and wondered what he was doing and why he was not doing other things. They wondered, at times, if he existed. They questioned many things – the afterlife and why God did not seem to heal and intervene in the many painful situations of life. They did not question their own calling to the priesthood or the fact that it was God calling them to this work. Underneath any stress they may have suffered, and several of them had suffered a great deal, there was a confident and quiet faith that believed God cared and would not let go of them. They appeared to have a confident faith. One said, 'Either God is or he isn't. I live dangerously with God and ask dangerous questions, and peer into the abyss. It is a necessary place to stay with God. I study the Masters and the Mystics and I'm not afraid of total darkness.'

Coping

Those in this category appeared to have a confident faith but with more doubts. Some of them were only just coping. Their doubts were not causing them to sink, but during interviews it felt as though it was a struggle for some of them to hold on.

1. An intellectual Faith

A single priest said, 'I have to believe God is there and he exists. My faith is intellectual rather than experiential, as I have not had a one-to-one encounter. I am an agnostic. I find God in the beauty, in music and the landscape. I believe if I did lose my faith I could go and talk to the bishop.'

This single priest said that he had lost his faith when he was 17, and he didn't believe in God at that time. 'It was associated with depression, and I did wonder then if I had the psychological stamina to be a priest. It is very frightening because if I lose faith, I lose job, house, everything. I had a period of depression in my last job. I doubted my own salvation, but I have learned to be more open and honest.'

This priest appeared to live on the edge. It felt as though he was just coping when interviewed.

2. An Incarnate Faith

A priest said, 'I've never lost faith in God. I do have doubts about

190

God and eternity. Sometimes it's hard to believe there is a God who created everything but then I see what God does in people's lives and it is staggering. God achieves fantastic things through people who are open to him and respond to him and do his will. I just want to proclaim the Gospel.'

This priest had experienced divorce and the feeling of failure that his broken marriage had given him.

3. A Nurturing Faith

A female priest said, 'I escape into spirituality from the frustrations of Church structures and I ask God to feed me. I've never experienced a loss of faith.' However, she experienced the 'hierarchy as abysmal'. Her faith and God were an escape from people who had let her down. Coping, for this priest, was about being able to find a safe place.

4. A Doubting Faith

One priest said, 'I don't know what it feels like *not* to believe in God but I do question the sanity of the whole Christian enterprise. Faith always comprises doubts and criticisms. I don't know what it is to hate God. Occasionally the Church gets in the way of God.'

Another priest, whose wife was very ill, said, 'God, where are you? Why don't you help? You've always come up with the goods before.' He said, 'I felt lost and abandoned but God did carry me through, though I didn't realise it.'

One priest said, 'God is there, however lousy life is. I've never lost faith. There's been a lot of crying out, "Father why have you dumped me like this?" I shout at God and throw things around.'

Another said, 'I have experienced a loss of faith. Faith is a gift from God and if I have it I mustn't take it for granted but sometimes my trust goes. That's the reason for having regular prayer times and to keep the windows open and keep something going even if the desert is all around. I have lots of doubts. I get them particularly when I look in the mirror and ask myself what I have done today that makes any sense. I shout at God in Church but I've never felt like giving up, as I can't give up on God.'

5. A Good Friday Faith

Some clergy described themselves as 'Good Friday' people, experiencing in their lives the sacrificial life of Christ. One priest said, 'I am an Easter person but I can't get that on the cheap without the cross. Priesthood involves taking up the cross. It is an awesome burden being a representative figure of the divine God. It has something to do with dying in order to live. Though I lost my faith when a teenager, I haven't since I was ordained. I keep asking God to remind me if he wants me to do the work, but if not, to let me know and let me off the hook. I have lost faith in the Church. I take all situations to God.'

6. An Act of Will

Many of the clergy had had traumatic experiences and yet had been able to remain connected to God.

One said, 'I see my trust in God as a marriage and I have never let go of that from the beginning of my ministry. I put my hand in God's hand when I was 18 and I won't withdraw it. It is an act of will and I have never wavered from the fact that I believe Jesus is the Son of God, and that he's gone through hell to prove his love for me. I offer depression and everything to God and say, "It's over to you." I try and turn it into prayers for those who do not know God.' This priest's son was killed very tragically when about 19 years old.

He continued, 'I feel frequently that God is a million miles away, so I snarl at him and feel he bloody well doesn't come up to expectations – and why the hell not! I feel he is too busy. I swear at God as it does less damage than swearing at my wife.'

When his son died he said, 'Things really came together. There was such overwhelming love from people across the board. Divisions were broken down and there was a real immense tide of prayer, which was very precious to us. I felt close to God and my wife, and God made a difference to us in ways that were really wonderful. I felt I'd come to terms with the reality of God and the reality of faith.'

7. Transitional Symbols

One clergyman had doubts about doctrines of the creed: 'I wonder in the Eucharist if this is just a bit of bread I'm holding up. The whole thing seems so bizarre. I sometimes think God is not listening and is not paying a blind bit of notice. I shout and swear at God frequently.'

Discussion

The difference between the coping clergy and the confident clergy is only in degrees. The confident clergy said they had never thought of giving up. They had not lost their faith, though they questioned God and did have doubts. The coping clergy had, at times, felt like giving up. Their doubts appeared more severe and they had a greater need to shout at God. Though they had thought of giving up, they had not done so. There was enough sense of the transcendental to enable them to feel still attached to the Divine.

Doubting

It could be said that those clergy experiencing real doubts have reasons to do so, like the two clergy who, at the time of the interviews, had just been deserted by their wives. One other was experiencing profound depression, having had to move from his previous parish due to the appointment of an ordained woman priest. There is evidence to suggest that such profound stress correlates with severe doubts about faith. The two clergy whose wives had left had lost not only a spouse, but a support structure as well.

1. A Changing Faith

The priest who was opposed to the ordination of women as were many others, found it hard to understand how his world had been so profoundly changed. As he said, 'Leaving my last parish I went through a dark night of the soul. The stress was real and palpable. In order to try and overcome this stress I try and look for God in beauty and creation.' He had been able to paint his dark night of the soul.

Both clergy whose wives left had suffered breakdowns. One said, 'God and I have ongoing battles. We have for years. I just don't want to do things God tells me to do. My battle is, how do I cope?'

2. A Distant God

One priest said, 'I go through times of doubting and wonder if God is present. He is very distant and I wonder if there is any point in doing what I am doing. I wonder if God is out there. I didn't feel him there at the height of my breakdown.'

One priest who had experienced ill health, said, 'I wonder if it's all a load of rubbish, though I have never lost my faith. My framework of daily offices and the Eucharist gives me a scaffolding to support me. I don't totally give up on praying as my duty as a priest keeps me going.'

One priest said, 'I have lots of doubts but I've not lost faith – but I'm not sure what it is anyway, as it is very elusive.'

Another priest said, 'I wondered where God was at Mass on Sunday. I've never lost faith.'

Listening to these clergy there was so much pathos in their disclosures. Their experience was very near the two clergy who, at the time of interview, were experiencing disbelief.

Disbelief

One expressed the Church, himself and the New Testament as being irrelevant to people. He said, 'I feel my spiritual well is dry. The Eucharist no longer communicates to me. I have crossed over from being quiet with God to being lonely. I wonder if prayer and meditation really work.'

It was very hard for this priest to talk about God at all. There did seem a direct link, however, with the fact that he had initially come into ministry through his admiration for certain other priests he had met or whose books he had read. In his interview his faith did not appear to have the experiential quality of others. His failed first marriage, and the illness and depression he was suffering when interviewed, all added to his sense of despair.

Nothing appeared to bear any signs of hope for him – certainly not the Church or Christianity.

The other priest appeared more buoyant. He openly talked of his 'loss of faith'. Though he was worried about the effects of it on his work, his home and his future, he was excited at what he may discover. 'It is creative. The death of my father four years ago, and working through my feelings about him, have allowed me to let go of my faith. I'm not sure what will take its place – whether orthodox Christianity or something else.' God as a father figure was no longer needed. He had, however, nothing to put in its place.

Discussion

For both of these clergy God appeared to be dead. Not only could they not 'see' or 'experience' God in their lives, but it also appeared as though any faith they had had was a mirage; promising a lot, but without any substance. All the expectations of their 'call' to the priesthood had been burned in the fire of their disappointment that the Christian faith itself had seemingly nothing left to offer them.

Conclusion

This theory question looked at the heart of the psychological needs of the clergy. Within the exploration of their emotional and spiritual health the cracks were clearly visible. Those clergy whose faith was seen to be a living, dynamic experience appeared to cope emotionally. It also appeared that those who were emotionally strong enjoyed a vibrant spiritual life. They dared to express their doubts but it did not deter them from trusting in a God they could not see. They appeared strong and buoyed up.

The questions probed the inner world of the clergy, exposing in a way no other question had, their fears and vulnerabilities. It was not surprising that the clergy spoke of needing to feel supported. Several clergy expressed their disaffection with hierarchical support. They felt need for affirmation and encouragement for the work they had done; this did not happen. In spite of this, being a priest appeared to be compensation enough, especially if they found fulfilment in their spiritual communion with God. Then they felt fed and nurtured.

Support was a key word. The support of partners, colleagues and the hierarchy. Those who experienced such caring relationships tended to have come from secure backgrounds. If not, they had managed to integrate and work through the emotional traumas of the past. The clergy who, whilst expressing doubts about their faith, yet had a lively relationship with God, appeared to see the Almighty as outside rather than as an internal parental figure. Those whose God seemed made in the image of past significant figures, found they had 'grown out of' the need for such a relationship.

Clergy experiencing extreme trauma due to break-up of their marriages or deep depression found it hard to hold on to a loving God who cared for them. It was at these crisis points that there appeared a sense of desperation and a need to know the Bishop was there and cared.

In exploring this last section it became clear that outside opinion, coupled with the lack of internal integration, affected the 'clergy's work, their own spiritual journey and every aspect of their life'. These findings support the three hypotheses that were initially suggested.

Chapter 8: Who cares for the carers?

Pastors for the clergy

Charlotte Elliott's hymn 'Just as I am' encapsulates the reality of life lived out by every respondent in this research project. However impenetrable the masks for their congregations, the clergy knew the truth of the words 'Just as I am'. In the glare of their public parochial life, the privacy of their homes and the hidden depths of their souls open to God, they can only be who and what they are – vulnerable always, weak at times, and full of pain on occasion.

This whole enterprise was threaded through with themes of pain. My own fear of failure as a researcher found an echo in the heart of many of the clergy as they spoke about their inadequacies.

This research produced a real dilemma. This had occurred between reporting and analysing as honestly as possible the sense of pain and the lack of supportive care many of the respondents had shared and the position of the bishops. Bishops now occupy very high-profile public roles. Some have become international spokesmen for the Church of England and world-wide Anglicanism, as well as national figures. This creates enormous pressure and places strain on their office. It also militates against their being able to sustain a personal pastoral role with all the clergy in their diocese. Much of this work has now been delegated to other senior clergy, such as archdeacons, though bishops still retain the desire and commitment to be the chief pastor of their clergy.

It is not surprising, therefore, that though the will to pastor is there, the perception of many clergy is that bishops are distant; even if they do care, they have no real time to be personally involved in their welfare. This was heard throughout the research project. There were, however, other clergy who felt the pastoral care was perfectly adequate. They felt they only had to pick up the phone and they would be able to speak to their bishop about their concerns. It has to be said that these clergy managed parishes that appeared to be successful. They themselves came over as confident in the work they were doing, and felt fulfilled in all the areas of life examined. The clergy in the project who felt unsupported and uncared for seemed to experience severe difficulties in every aspect of their lives.

Married as I am, to a member of the senior clergy, I found myself feeling much sympathy for the bishops and their enormous workloads. I also, however, heard the clear voice of the clergy's anguish at the lack of care, and their need to be heard.

The parochial clergy were the focus of this research project, but in order to provide a sense of cohesion, the views of several other significant Church people were included. The two bishops of the dioceses where the research was carried out were interviewed, and imparted important information and insights to the questions asked (Appendix 4).

The Director of the Ministry Division, the Venerable Dr Gordon Kuhrt, was also interviewed (Appendix 5). The Ministry Division oversees the whole national selection process, the training and ongoing training of future clergy, and advises bishops on clergy remuneration and conditions of service. The director was able to provide an overview of the life of the clergy from their first contact with the institution until retirement.

Because training is vital it was important to interview a principal of a theological college, and Dr Christina Baxter, Principal of St John's Theological College, Nottingham, was chosen (Appendix 6). A well-known theologian, she is Chair of the House of Laity within the General Synod and a member of the Archbishop's Council.[1] Though attached to the evangelical wing of the Church she is widely respected, and has been involved with theological training for over 20 years.

I also visited and interviewed the wardens of three centres of healing; Burrswood, The Society of Mary and Martha, and the Dympna Centre. In various ways these places seek to offer space, counselling, time for spiritual reflection and the opportunity for

---

1 Executive Council of General Synod

clergy and Christian leaders to re-evaluate their ministry. The Church hierarchy may refer clergy to such centres during periods of crisis.

Themes from the Research

As stated in Chapter 1, six areas of the clergy's life were explored.

1. Why they were ordained
2. Whom they see as having authority over them
3. What being a priest means to them
4. Their family relationships
5. The type of leadership they exercise
6. Their spiritual and emotional health

Several themes emerged from what the clergy had to say. These themes of irrelevance, isolation, despair, guilt and low self-esteem affected their work, spiritual journey and every aspect of their life.

1. Irrelevance

One theme that recurred throughout this research, especially in the southern diocese, was that of the irrelevance of the Church. The Church had great difficulty in reaching out to the unchurched, the disinterested and the disadvantaged. Though many clergy opened their churches during the time of national mourning for Princess Diana in August 1997 and the terrorist atrocity on 11 September in New York, and found them briefly full, they were unable to capitalise on that to any great extent, and the churches soon returned to their normally small congregations.

From the whole sample of 236 churches, only 20 had congregations of over 150 people. Many had congregations with fewer than 50 people attending each week. Ministering week by week to a handful of people can be very disheartening if it continues for long enough.

2. Isolation

The continuing feelings of being irrelevant led to a sense of isolation. This was experienced in different ways. Several clergy spoke of being unable to make friends within the community – 'Who would want to be friends with a priest?' Living in different housing, working from home (even though this is more fashionable in the twenty-first century), and working for an institution that was often pilloried by the press, had alienated them from the rest of society. This was exacerbated if they had transgressed.

Clergy whose spouses have left the marriage are offered much supportive care from the hierarchy, even if that is not always experienced as such, but it is often more difficult for the senior staff when the clergy themselves have erred. Here the split between the ideal of the Church and the 'messiness' of the reality are clearly visible. Clergy who had themselves 'stepped out of line' described how hard it had been to be reinstated. They saw a Gospel that is about forgiveness and restoration, and wondered why that could not be applied in their case.

The bishop from the north spoke about the code of practice in operation in such an event. A structural discipline would include seeing 'a counsellor unconnected to me, and having spiritual direction . . . with a view to reintroduction to ministry'. Though the process, from a bishop's point of view, is fairly clear, it did not always appear so from the transgressor's angle. Clergy in such a position, when they have lost their home, stipend and job, felt isolated and neglected as they sought to put their life back together.

In many ways the above highlights the experienced difference between being in secular employment or in that of the Church. Being ordained is about difference. It is about aloneness whilst offering an often uninterested community a Gospel of repentance and restoration. Faced with such a task, it is not surprising that many feel not just daunted, but also isolated from others.

3. Despair

Real despair was seen in very few of the clergy. Where it was apparent it was mainly because of a difficult life event they were negotiating. Others expressed times of despair, often equated with spiritual and physical malaise. The Principal of St John's Theological College, Nottingham, said, 'I try to help people understand that physical, spiritual and emotional health are all interwoven and if you don't give attention to all of them, each or all may suffer.' The clergy who struggled had experienced, and were experiencing, various physical illnesses and or emotional traumas. That this affected their spiritual life was not in the least surprising.

Suffering from despair exacerbates the feeling of being out of control. Clergy who feel unable to carry on lose everything: their home, income and job. This only adds to the sense of desperation.

4. Guilt

Most of the clergy expressed at some time throughout the interviews their feeling that they did not do enough. One expressed it graphically when saying that at night, as he reviewed the day, he never felt that what he had accomplished had been right. He always felt he should have managed the things he hadn't achieved.

The problem of guilt produced, they said, a constant need for reassurance and affirmation, which was why it was so crucial that clergy felt supported by their partners and by the hierarchy. Several clergy stated that they could not manage without their wives. The single clergy expressed their need for close friends or colleagues to provide that sort of reassurance.

5. Low Self-esteem

There is much that will militate against a sense of pride in the ministry. Constant denigration by the press, or a lack of care from a sometimes disaffected laity, produces feelings of lack of self worth. Many of the clergy came into the ministry with a clear call from God but from backgrounds of emotional deprivation. As a result of this they had a deep need to find a sense of self. The image and uniform of the priest provided this in large measure. The reality, however, often probed beyond the mask and exposed

201

the raw nerves beneath. Feelings of inadequacy, being out of control, fear, and not knowing what they were doing, were expressed; the latter especially from the young, who had recently been made Incumbents. Much of ministry is about getting on and finding out about the job themselves. One of the clergy lamented the fact that he had not been given a job description before he started.

Besides these negative themes many positive ones were also expressed. It was apparent that many of the clergy felt fulfilled within their work. When discussing the difference between the apparently successful clergy and those who fail, the southern Bishop said that success was not just to do with spirituality. He said, 'The Church is looking for leadership skills . . . an entrepreneurial "get up and go-ness" that often sorts out one priest from another.' The northern bishop also used the word 'entrepreneur'. Both felt that 'successful' clergy were those who were able to get into the community, make contact and reach people where they were. They needed to be innovative and creative.

It is, however, the emotional needs of all the clergy that are under the microscope. Because they are human and fallible, all of them will have needs that require care and support. The negative themes from the research highlighted those needs. How can they be met?

Response of the Hierarchy

In discussing the needs of the clergy with the two bishops and Gordon Kuhrt and Christina Baxter, all four felt these needs could be met under three categories: care of clergy, codes of practice, and continuing ministerial education.

1. Care of clergy

Dr Baxter discussed the care and attention theological colleges direct towards the ordinand's whole person, including the family. There was plenty of opportunity throughout the course for the ordinands to discover about their own human growth and development. They had opportunities for ongoing counselling, and much time and energy was devoted to the ordinand's spouse, in order to enable both of them to come to terms with living in a clergy house, and all that entails. Where there were grave problems, students or their spouses were referred for psychiatric help and pastoral care. It was also true that the above provisions were not available at all theological colleges, though every effort was being made to provide such facilities.

Dr Baxter was well aware of the pressures that parochial life presented. She cited cases where students of hers, now in parochial ministry, had 'got into difficulties and made a shipwreck of their faith and marriage'. She said it was not always their fault. She gets angry when the diocese does absolutely nothing to help them. 'I know that because they come crying to me.'

Both bishops said that a lot of supportive care is happening though it is 'often crisis management'. Dr Kuhrt spelled it out clearly. He felt that the care of the clergy should consist of:

a. Care at the local level through shared ministry with the laity and local ordained colleagues.

b. Easy access to the bishop and his advisers when there are problems.

c. Specialist help, psychotherapy, spiritual direction or medical advice, easily available.

There does appear to be a real desire on the part of all concerned to try to address the needs of the clergy.

2. Codes of Practice

Dr Baxter said that many clergy are 'extraordinarily naïve about sexuality and on the whole don't have the kind of framework of teaching that would help them handle difficult issues'. She went on to say that this was exacerbated because clergy and their spouses were very loath to ask for help. They seldom did until there was a crisis, when it was often too late to resolve anything.

General Synod and many dioceses are increasingly producing

codes of good practice for their clergy, in order to help them manage more effectively the boundaries needed in their relationships with people. Many clergy marriages have broken down because a priest has been too zealous in the care of the bereaved and has not been aware of the inherent dangers of intimacy. It is within such relationships of pain and hurt that, often unawares, the clergy seek to meet their own needs of affirmation in offering inappropriate care and comfort.

3. Continuing Ministerial Education

Dr Baxter was very direct about the need for each person to be responsible for their own continuing learning and psychological growth. Both bishops and Dr Kuhrt talked about the Continuing Ministry Education programmes that many dioceses offer to all their clergy. These comprise interviews with senior staff on a regular basis, sometimes every 18 months, for review or appraisal of their work, and an exploration of the possibilities for future ministry. This is linked to resources for in-service training.

In the north there was a brochure which helped clergy plan this for themselves, together with a check-list. Clergy were also encouraged to meet in triads or in twos, depending on the diocese, though this met with a mixed reception as clergy find it hard to share openly and honestly with their peers.

In many dioceses clergy are recommended to find a consultant, supervisor or mentor with whom they can discuss the intricacies and diversity of their job. Few avail themselves of this opportunity, and so pass by the possibility of exploring in practical ways how to cope with the vagaries of their ministry.

Listening to the response of these senior members of the Church, it was obvious that there was a great deal of concern for the welfare of the clergy. The rising number of clergy marriage breakdowns, and the often visible distress of the clergy, had provoked the hierarchy into looking at ways of addressing their needs. Yet for all that is being offered, it still appears to many clergy that it is not enough. Is it because the reasons for the clergy's distress are not something that can be easily remedied?

Like the rest of humanity, the clergy are caught up in a consumerist culture that has little time or space for the transcendental. Added to this is the advent of women ordained to the priesthood, and the ripples thus caused.

In reading through the three hypotheses in the Introduction, how the clergy managed the changing culture appears to depend 'more on their own internal emotional strength and ego identity', as the third hypothesis suggested.

Much thought is directed towards caring for the ordained 'workforce'. As well as their own spiritual maturity, the emotional needs of the clergy must not be forgotten. A female priest married to a male priest said, 'He and I work on the assumption that our health and well-being are entirely our responsibility before God. We assume nothing will come from outside. We do not expect the parishioners to care for us or to even think we have needs. It is very liberating for us to have got there.' That, maybe, is the case for them. For many others their emotional deprivation prevents them from handling their needs in such a mature way, and it is the needs of such clergy that most need to be taken into consideration.

Implications for Psychotherapy or Counselling

Having reflected on the data gathered, it became very clear that the main area of concern for the clergy is to do with conflict. This has been highlighted at several levels.

External Conflict

1. The conflict engendered through believing in and proclaiming a message in which the encompassing culture seemingly has little interest.

2. The conflict between fulfilling a role that the Church appears to value, but which the community fails to understand. Many clergy were often asked if they worked only on a Sunday.

3. The conflict between being accountable to an authority that on the one hand offers pastoral oversight but on the other hand appears aloof and distant.

4. The conflict in being the 'professional', who dispenses the faith to an increasingly theologically educated laity, who do not always affirm the clergy's expertise. There appeared to be a noticeable hostility in many churches between clergy and laity. The anecdotal expectations of the laity have appeared to rise in proportion to the decline in church attendance.

5. The conflict produced through attending to what feels like the never-ending demands of the parishioners, and balancing this with the needs of family life.

6. The conflict of living in tied accommodation often totally at variance with the surrounding dwellings.

7. The conflict inherent in living in a 'goldfish bowl'.

Internal Conflict

1. Many clergy expressed the feeling that they were unable to meet everyone's needs. The feeling of failure and guilt at never accomplishing the task was a constant internal conflict.

2. Preaching about a life that demands that the leader be 'above reproach, the husband of one wife, temperate, self-controlled, respectable, hospitable . . .' (1 Timothy 3:2), whilst struggling with the inner realities of their own natural inclinations. That this produced enormous conflict was graphically expressed by those whose marriages had broken down.

3. Preaching a message that was no longer tenable for that priest. Many expressed such conflicts, and all the clergy admitted to having doubts at various times. It was when these doubts formed into a different belief-system that the inner turmoil became almost impossible to bear.

4. The clergy had a need to feel affirmed by the congregation but also by the hierarchy. When this was not forthcoming they felt hurt. This led to feelings of anger at the bishops, whom they felt did not accept the role of 'Father in God'.

5. The almost unconscious awareness of gender issues, now that women are ordained as priests, was barely recognised or

acknowledged by most male clergy, yet from the data it appeared that this was of major concern to them, however it was expressed.

6. The conflict that was inherent especially in those from emotionally deprived backgrounds, who struggled daily to feel 'good enough'. Their battle with the 'demons within' were acted out in various ways, such as inappropriate contact with people, in order to assuage their need for love.

These external and internal conflicts, if unmanageable, are all indications of the need for counselling. Most dioceses and Bishops provide the opportunity for such help. Centres like Burrswood in Kent and The Society of Mary and Martha near Exeter offer a safe place away from parish pressures to work through some of the issues highlighted.

Suggestions for Future Research

1. There appears to be a need to look more closely at 'why' men and women wish to be ordained. Many of those who have been seem to have very fragile identities. Is that why they gravitate towards a seemingly safe institution?

2. More research should look at the meaning of priesthood for the clergy. They joined a religious dogma but became part of a workforce. In doing so they are saying, 'Define me, hold me, keep me safe'. That it did not do so was for them shocking and desperately sad. Instead, the clergy experienced a real sense of dislocation, as they juggled being in the world with not forming part of that world's cultural ethos.

3. The area of authority needs to be carefully looked at, both from the bishops' and the clergy's perspective. Some bishops exercise their role more autocratically, whilst others undertake a far more egalitarian partnership with their priests. Is that to do with the bishops' personal psychological agendas, the dictates of the whole Church or the apparent needs of the

clergy? There can be little doubt that, just as the priest sets the tone for the Church within a community, so does the Bishop within his own diocese.

4. Because relationships are at the heart of ministry, more research needs to be done on them at all levels:
   - Family relationships and how they affect the clergy. Many couples now are both ordained priests, so that there are various different combinations within the clergy household.
   - Relationships between clergy and congregations.
   - Relationships between clergy and other clergy, especially in the deanery setting. This would provide interesting data concerning envy and competitiveness among clergy.

5. More work needs to be done in order to explore the link between emotional and spiritual health. It appeared within the data that there is a direct association between the clergy's feelings of disappointment, disenchantment or experiences of betrayal, and their loss of faith. It would be interesting to investigate whether the possibility of a loss of faith could be predicted at the selection stage. That may only happen if there is a greater appreciation of the candidate's background.

The opportunities for more research are legion, whilst the need for such a task is clear to see. Meanwhile, the clergy from these two dioceses, working at the coalface of their societies, were the ones whose stories have been told within these pages. Their needs were embedded in the opening phrase of the hymn, 'Just as I am'.

Conclusion

As I reflect two years later on this project that I undertook, several general conclusions came to mind. These have been informed over the years by my work as a Bishop's Selector, Bishop's Visitor and now as a member of General Synod. Observations as a psychotherapist and marital therapist, and the fact that I am a practising Christian, have also reinforced these ideas.

Clergy

Clergy need to remind themselves that they have been called by God, to this holy work, but that it has been ratified by the whole Church. As such they are accredited, set apart, and ordained through the laying on of a bishop's hands. This calling is not to perfection, but to openness to God's grace being poured out through them. Clergy need to keep reminding themselves that God can use their weakness and vulnerability and work through it, just as Jesus did with his disciples. The cracks they feel can be used as openings of blessing, both to them and through them.

Laity

Congregations must learn not to have unreasonable expectations of their clergy. Looking at any parish profile during an interregnum as a parish seeks a new incumbent is a daunting task. Parishes want the 'perfect priest' and often feel very let down when they find the person in the vicarage or rectory is just like them. It is only the love and grace of God that changes us. Laity have a responsibility to love and care for their clergy, just as much as they expect them to care for their flock. We are all in the ministry together, and need each other's love and affirmation.

Bishops

It is always exciting to see a lively, dynamic Incumbent move the Church on, so that it becomes a beacon of light in the greyness of much parish work. Most clergy are ordinary people simply wanting to do the work they believe God has called them to. It is not helpful to them when they feel the hierarchy expect more of them than they can deliver, and only adds to the burden of not feeling 'good enough'. However important it is for bishops to be involved in international and national affairs, diocesan bishops are still the chief pastors of the clergy. They have a primary role in helping the clergy to feel valued and affirmed. Clergy need to know their bishop cares about and is interested in them and in what they are doing, and not just when things are going awry. Much of the bishop's pastoral work can be put into effect by the archdeacons, spiritual directors, mentors, supervisors and the diocesan training staff. But it is no less true that the clergy need to feel they can have easy access to their bishop, and that the bishop will have time for them.

However, bishops, priests, deacons and laity alike are fallible human beings. Each have their own stories to tell from their childhood which reverberate in their adult interactions. Jesus' injunction to 'love one another as I have loved you' (John 15:12), is a more imperative command than ever before. We live in a world full of suspicion, with cultural hatred very near the surface and little respect for the needs and concerns of others. The Christian Gospel, with its emphasis on love, acceptance and grace, must be lived out and experienced within the clerical profession so that it can be spread out within congregations and the communities around.

Chapter 9: The end?

Treasures in jars of clay

Fairy tales finish 'happily ever after'. Research which explores people's lives, and the culture within which they work, can have no such easy ending. As I write, the USA, Britain and the rest of the world is coping with the aftermath of the horrific destruction by terrorists of the World Trade Centre 'Twin Towers' in New York and part of the Pentagon in Washington, on 11 September 2001. The reverberations of such horrendous crimes will affect not just the West, but the whole of the world for years to come. The clergy themselves will be faced with ministering to frightened and bewildered communities as questions are asked about where God is in all this horror.

When such evil becomes so visible, it may be that the Church, which proclaims Jesus as the Light of the World, will no longer be irrelevant and ignored. It may be that now the clergy will be better able to reach out to the needy and fearful, with confidence in the Gospel of salvation.

The clergy in this research knew what it meant to feel weak and vulnerable. Their fragility was highlighted many times, as was the fact that their primary way of coping had been to turn to the source of their predicament, God. Having been called to the ordained ministry, they now looked to him to provide answers.

From the material generated by the research, certain conclusions were looked at in the previous chapter, and it was recognised that further in-depth research is needed. Perhaps that is how it should be, for research is like a pilgrimage. The road ahead is unclear, and only gradually unfolds. There are many surprises on the way and several areas of tough terrain to be negotiated. Stumbling frequently along the way, with much fear at times, I have found, as Eliot did, that 'the end of all our exploring will be to arrive where we started, and know the place for the first time'.

The aim of this research was to analyse the clergy's view of the problems and conflicts they confronted in their lives.

It was by investigating their perception of their life and work that an answer would be found as to whether the clergy perceived themselves as 'successful' or 'failures'. That depended more on their own internal integration than on the lack of credibility of the Christian faith to the surrounding community.

The aim was also to explore the relationship between the institution of the Church and the life of the ordained clergy.

All of the clergy were prepared to give their time to discuss their feelings and perceptions of the six areas to be explored – why they were ordained, what was their view of authority, what it meant to them to be a priest, their personal relationships, their work within their parishes, and their emotional and spiritual health. The data from the interviews became the voice of the clergy and it was this voice that produced answers as to whether the hypotheses were borne out.

One priest expressed throughout his interview his feeling that people are no longer interested in God: 'The Gospel is irrelevant and so am I.' In many ways, he exemplified those priests whose confidence in the Christian message had disintegrated beneath the wave of liberalism within society, and the negative media attention given to the Church.

The clergy who were most affected by the loss of Christian belief and standards in the wider society were those who found their work, spiritual journey and every aspect of their life affected. The aloneness of the priest who said, 'no one wants to talk to a priest', expressed the sense of alienation felt by some clergy. Their loss of self-esteem as a minister of the Gospel was experienced by some as clinical depression and by others as a loss of faith. Whatever the expression of their dis-ease, it was felt in every area of their life. The priest who claimed to have lost his faith also expressed the ambivalence of not being able to do anything about it, because it would mean he would lose his job, his pension and his home. The only option open to him was to live a lie.

There were several clergy who had openly faced the modern-day culture. They had also faced their own vulnerability and fear of failure, and one had openly shared his homosexuality with his parish. Though he had experienced many times of 'crucifixion' in the past, he now depended on an internal emotional strength which emerged as he became more integrated. It was this integration of his fragility that allowed him and others to minister confidently within their recognised and acknowledged weakness.

The research was first and last about the men and women who had heard God's call to the ordained Anglican ministry. Some had been prepared to leave lucrative and powerful jobs to obey that call. Others had found coming into the Anglican ministry had provided them with a status, and a middle-class way of life which would have seemed impossible apart from ordination. Whether they had moved from poverty to seeming wealth, riches to poverty, or from one status to another, the clergy all spoke of the change that had occurred for them and their families through the choices they had made. It was their obedience to the call that changed everything.

What sort of people are prepared for such an upheaval, and the effect it would have on them and their families? To answer this question it is important to look back over the pilgrimage of the research and to understand the anthem that accompanied me on the journey.

Looking from afar at the Church of England, the clergy and their relationships had the semblance of looking at a cracked pot. The Church of England has lost not only its power base within the country but also, as has been seen, much respect, in part due to its vacillation on doctrinal and moral issues. Though still involved in the ceremonial life of Great Britain, and with its Bishops still sitting in the House of Lords, its influence on the day to day life of vast numbers of the population is nevertheless minimal. Historically, through its buildings, the Church of England is still a recognised institution, but barely 2 per cent of the population now attend services on a regular basis.

The brokenness of the institution has affected its workforce. In many instances the clergy have lost confidence in their bishops, in the Church and even, at times, in the message they proclaim. This gradual erosion of certainties has occurred through sociological change, but also because of internal strife within the church.

The impact of ordination to the priesthood of women was perceived to be of earthquake proportions, affecting not only those who were opposed to its implementation. It had, and continues to have, Richter scale effects within the Church of England. Once completely male-dominated and male-led, this ancient institution is experiencing a 'sex change'.

Many able women are being ordained priest; as their numbers increase so the landscape will change, due to the different insight and perspectives they bring. The cracks will widen as women, who once appeared to be second-class Christians, are now beginning to be heard with a priestly voice in the corridors of power.

These changes are far-reaching in their effects, and these may be compounded if and when General Synod approves the consecration of female priests as bishops, or the ordination of practising homosexuals.

The fear of a fragmenting Church or a fragmented clergy, appeared like a motif running through this research.

The cracked pot

In 2 Corinthians 4:7-12 St Paul gives a vivid description of the stresses and strains of Christian ministry. He describes the minister as 'hard pressed on every side, but not crushed' (verse 8), and contrasts this with the almighty power of God, who works within the human heart, which he eloquently describes as a 'jar of clay'. This vivid illustration is of the kind of ordinary clay pot which would have been used as a kitchen utensil on an everyday basis in Paul's time. Yet this common jar is both the container of the priceless treasure of God's grace, and at the same time battered and cracked by everything thrown at it from the surrounding culture. Paul can therefore say that Christians, both in his day and ours, 'carry around in our own body the death of the Lord Jesus, so that the life of Jesus may also be revealed in our body' (verse 10).

214

The research clearly shows the pressures that batter the emotions and the souls of the clergy in the present day, causing scars, and often cracks in the human 'jars of clay'. When linked with Jeremiah's famous passage (Jeremiah 18:4), these words of St Paul remind us that not only will the Master Potter reshape the pot, but also that if allowed, his love and grace can be the healing ointment pouring through the cracks of the vulnerable clergy to minister wholeness to a broken and hurting world.

Those who offer themselves to God's service for full-time ordained ministry have at the time just a brief glimpse of what responding to his call might cost them in terms of the effects, both on their own lives and on those whom they love. Most of those who took part in the research felt the rewards they experienced far outweighed the prices they sometimes had to pay.

The following poem encapsulates well the trauma of having been broken. It also describes the grace and love of the Master Potter as he reshapes the clay so that he can use it. Many of the clergy testified to such an experience of 'new birth'.

Broken

'It lay in fragments, shattered, broken, marred:
the vessel crushed – its beauty torn apart.
The pattern that had formed its outer glory
    in dust and splinters split upon the ground.
The shape it once had held lay there no more –
    the etched design of years we'd grown to know –
    the potter's handiwork returned to nought,
    lay fractured, rudely scattered on the earth.

Anguish held me and torment choked my soul;
    the agony of brokenness – the pain,
    the severing of the known, the shadows of the past
    grief overwhelmed me, shook me as I cried.

The hidden inner parts were now displayed,
    a myriad pieces in the seeing light,

their covering, a mask, was swept away;
    unveiled, their shame and torture laid to view.
Some trod that way and trampled underfoot
    or threw aside the remnants as they passed;
    yet others would deride the crumpled flask
    seeing no beauty in the scattered clay.

Yet in the desperation of my heart
    I see the Potter, weeping, stooping down;
    gently he cradles the fragments, lifting them close,
    not one is missed, each piece is sought and held.

My precious workmanship, the pleasure of my hands
    I fashioned you and gave you life and form;
    how is your beauty scarred, your tenderness exposed,
    who plundered the secret places of your heart?
Who savaged the love I planted deep within?
Bruised and rejected you brought sorrow, tears?
Such pain I see, torment and misery,
    deep, dark despair – yet you were made for joy!
You were not made to bear this heavy load;
    you have been crushed – but you are in my hands.

The Master Potter gently took each piece,
    and built again a vessel as he chose.
Its shape was softer than before – its tracing fine,
    he breathed his healing love to seal each join;
    it was a patient work, he did not rush
    to force the fractured remnants into place,
    but held each one until the pain had ebbed,
    then quietly joined them in his new design.

I felt the newness of the Maker's touch
    and saw with wonder how he brought again
    a treasure, fashioned to his glorious plan;
    a new creation, out of brokenness.
He held it now with pleasure in his eyes,

yes, and with love and set it in its place.
'You have come through the fire, my little one,
  you have been ravaged – now you're made anew,
  rejoice to me my child born out of love,
  and know that I was broken once – for you'.
Sue Wharton, 24 February 1991

Brokenness, fragmentation and cracked pots are a theological, as well as a psychological metaphor. Throughout the Bible in both Old and New Testaments, the people of God are seen to fragment through disobedience to God's law and absorption into a heathen culture. However, this very brokenness provides a seed of hope. Not only from a poetic, but also from a theological point of view, it could be said the Master Potter is at work to mend and repair. It is for this reason that the clergy first discovered a faith for themselves. It is also for this reason that the clergy felt they had something to say about it.

A cracked pot can be broken from inside or outside. Water freezing within and expanding may cause cracking. The roots of a plant pushing out may break the pot. Equally, weight or impact of any sort may destroy the pot from outside.

Within each member of the clergy there is the possibility of the stress from within (lack of belief, family pressures) or from without (parish expectations and hierarchical demands), fragmenting such a fragile vessel. A cracked pot may appear useless, unattractive. It can, however, be a thing of beauty. A lighted candle placed within a cracked pot will produce a diffused light. A cracked pot may adorn the top of a waterfall where the water seeps through the cracks at a gentle pace, irrigating the rock garden below. The life-giving light and water of Jesus not only brings healing to the 'jar', but may be diffused out to bless all those around.

Such metaphors provide healing insights into the 'broken' Church or 'broken' priest. Each, if available, may be used for light to shine or water to flow through the cracked and broken parts, and so reach far beyond their own pain to enhance the lives of others. The visibility of the humanity of the clergy, exposed in doubt and frailty, may become a stream of healing within the lives of their congregation and community. The laity may then feel that the clergy now understand the struggles they wrestle with, most especially now within a crisis-ridden world.

The analyst sees the possibility of integration out of the trauma of brokenness as the individuals accept and work through these once unacceptable parts of themselves.

The Christian sees in Christ's broken body and poured-out blood the possibility of salvation for all who embrace that salvific work. Though many of the clergy appeared broken and inadequate for the task, it was that very 'crackedness' that provided the possibility of hope.

Ultimately the Church strives not for worldly success but for a wholeness that comes through brokenness. The task of the Church and its hierarchy is to enable that to happen as effectively as possible.

Appendix 1: Central research question

What are the psychotherapeutic needs
of Anglican parochial clergy today?

Theory Question 1

What were the psychological reasons for coming into the ordained ministry?

Informant Questions

1. What was the main influence on you to become a parish priest?
   a) Have there been other clergy in your family?

2. How did your family feel about you being ordained?

Theory Question 2

Where does the priest see the focus of authority coming from?

Information Questions

1. Who has authority over you in ministry?
   a) To whom do you feel answerable?
   b) In what way does that affect your work?
   c) If you feel you are primarily answerable to the Church or the bishop, what role does God play in your work?
   d) How do you discern the will of God?

Theory Question 3

Does the clergy's understanding of what it means to be a priest affect their work and how they see themselves?

Informant Questions

1. Which words have the most meaning for you?

   Word or Sacrament

   Priest or Pastor

   Father or Reverend

   Mass or Holy Communion

   Table or Altar

2. In what positive and negative ways does your view of priesthood affect your ministry?

3. In what ways does your view of priesthood affect people's attitude to you?

4. In what ways does this affect your relationship with God?

Theory Question 4

In what ways does the work of the incumbent affect your personal relationships?

Information Questions

1. How does your work as a priest affect your family?

2. How do you spend family time?

3. Has your partner's/family's attitude to your work changed over the years and, if so, how?

   a) Partner

   b) Family (i.e. children)

4. In what ways does the financial remuneration affect your lifestyle, if at all?

5. How does the work of a priest affect personal friendships?

Theory Question 5

Does the work of a priest produce transference/counter-transference situations and, if so, in what way?

Informant questions

1. In what ways did your training prepare you for the work of a priest?

2. What image do your parishioners have of you?

3. As you work with people do you find it provokes difficult feelings in you?

4. How do you handle people who expect more than you can give?

5. How do you maintain your professional boundaries?
   a) What would you do if you realised that a parishioner was sexually attracted to you?
   b) What would you do if you realised you were sexually attracted to a parishioner?

6. Are there aspects of your personal life which have been affected by perceived judgements from the outside world?

7. What do you do if a parishioner's needs overwhelm you?

Theory Question 6

Does the work of a priest affect his/her spiritual and mental health? If so, how?

Informant Questions

1. What does it mean to you to be a priest?

2. Have you suffered from stress and, if so, in what way?

3. Have you experienced a loss of faith? If so, how have you coped with doubt?

4. Have you experienced anger at times and, if so, how have you expressed it?

5. What has been the worst time of your ministry?
   a) Are there any areas in which you might like to receive more support?
   b) Have you ever felt like giving up?

6. What has been the best time in your ministry?

Appendix 2

A summary of the criteria for selection for ministry in the Church of England

1. Ministry within the Church of England

Candidates should be familiar with the tradition and practice of the Church of England and be ready to work within them.

2. Vocation

Candidates should be able to speak of their sense of vocation to ministry and mission, referring both to their own conviction and to the extent to which others have confirmed it. Their sense of vocation should be obedient, realistic and informed.

3. Faith

Candidates should show an understanding of the Christian faith and a desire to deepen their understanding. They should demonstrate personal commitment to Christ and a capacity to communicate the Gospel.

4. Spirituality

Candidates should show evidence of a commitment to a spiritual discipline, involving individual and corporate prayer and worship. Their spiritual practice should be such as to sustain and energise them in their daily lives.

5. Personality and character

Candidates should be sufficiently mature and stable to show that they are able to sustain the demanding role of a minister and to face change and pressure in a flexible and balanced way. They should be seen to be people of integrity.

6. Relationships

Candidates should demonstrate self-awareness and self-acceptance as a basis for developing open and healthy professional, personal and pastoral relationships as ministers. They should respect the will of the Church on matters of sexual morality.

7. Leadership and collaboration

Candidates should show ability to offer leadership in the Church community and to some extent in the wider community. This ability includes the capability to offer an example of faith and discipleship, to collaborate effectively with others, as well as to guide and shape the life of the Church community in its mission to the world.

8. Quality of mind

Candidates should have the necessary intellectual capacity and quality of mind to undertake satisfactorily a course of theological study and ministerial preparation and to cope with the intellectual demands of ministry.

Appendix 3

Five themes arising from servant leadership (see Chapter 4)

Sin

From childhood, Christians receive instruction in the main doctrinal beliefs of the Church. These centre around who God is and the human condition. They are taught that God is Creator, Saviour and Judge. Humankind, the highest point of God's creation, is seen to be flawed. Many believe, following St Augustine, that from the fall of Adam and Eve the human race has been affected by original sin. This sin 'introduces into the heart of human nature a limitation, a defect, that cannot be overcome by natural means' (Meissner, 1986, p. 221). Orthodox Christians will be aware of their inherent sinfulness 'since all have sinned and fall short of the glory of God' (Romans 3:23). Therefore 'all are born corrupt, because they are representatively incorporate in the sin and guilt of Adam . . . this is the root of each person's inherent disposition to sin . . . a person is not a sinner because he sins, he sins because he is a sinner' (Ferguson and Wright, 1988, p. 642).

Guilt

Each Christian will express in a variety of ways the feeling of letting God down, and from this comes a profound sense of guilt, because of feeling in 'the state of one who has committed a sin or a crime' (Ferguson and Wright, 1988, p. 285).

Guilt is 'a feeling of self-reproach resulting from a belief that one has done something wrong' (*The Collins Pocket Dictionary*, 1987). Meissner states that 'the phenomenon of guilt may reflect not only superego accusations but also a realist appraisal of moral failure by the ego' (Meissner, 1984, p. 131). Christians may feel a failure because they have, in some way, fallen short of what an omnipotent God requires.

Betrayal

Betrayal is defined as the failure 'to uphold . . . to desert' (*The Collins Pocket Dictionary*, 1987) the primary love object. As the perceived misdemeanour is explored, opened up and talked about with reference to the background and life in the family of origin, a sense of having betrayed God and parents will often be experienced. The fifth commandment, 'honour your father and your mother that your days may be long in the land which the Lord your God gives you' (Exodus 20:12), is an exhortation to all Christians. Daring to investigate the inadequacy of parental nurturing during childhood causes many metaphorically to look over their shoulder to see if God can see and hear.

The Christian priest moves from an awareness of having done wrong to a feeling of guilt for the offence, followed by a sense of betrayal, as they suggest that childhood deprivation by the care-givers may be one cause of their subsequent distress. Working through these feelings gradually enables that person to form a different perspective on past relationships, the traumas they have experienced, and the culpability of significant others in their life.

Doubt

Doubt is defined as 'to be uncertain or undecided . . . to be inclined to disbelieve' (*The Collins Pocket Dictionary*, 1987).

Among Evangelical Christians 'it is a popular misconception that doubt is tantamount to unbelief. In fact, although doubt may lead to unbelief it may equally produce a firmer faith' (Ferguson and Wright, 1988, p. 208).

Thomas, in the New Testament, is the archetypal doubter for Christians. He would not believe in the risen Jesus until he had seen him for himself and put his hand into the nail prints of Jesus' hands and feet.

For Christians, doubt takes many forms. As a result of experiencing the pain of suffering and loss, they may doubt the existence of a God who cares. They may feel the only God who is there is punitive and sadistic, with little interest in the inhabitants of his world – for what they read in the Bible, especially in the New Testament, bears little resemblance to their daily experience.

But doubt may also be about a desire to know more. 'Learning through radical questioning has been an important and accepted method of making progress in understanding' (Ferguson and Wright, 1988, p. 209). Thirdly, doubt may be experienced as losing faith held on to until now. This can feel both frightening and liberating, as people struggle to make a sense of their earlier concepts of God in the light of their greater internal awareness.

Wholeness

Wholeness represents a seeking after completeness, health, being 'not broken, damaged, defective, etc.' (*The Collins Pocket Dictionary*, 1987).

'The word health comes from the Old English root *hal*, which means whole, and from which the words wholeness and holiness are also derived' (Ferguson and Wright, 1988, p. 287). It can be seen that health and wholeness are almost synonymous. Jung stated that 'it is highly improbable that there could ever be a therapy that got rid of all difficulties. Man needs difficulties; they are necessary for health' (Campbell, 1971, p. 278). However, his aim in treatment was to enable his patients to go through a healing process to what he called the individuation process, which he believed is 'an identification with the totality of the personality, with the self' (Jung, 1968, p. 138). This is the ability to integrate the unacceptable aspects of the self.

Many clergy struggle with their doubts about God, about themselves and the perception of the world around, then gradually a working through to the realisation 'that it is possible to make sense of life' (Van Deurzen-Smith, 1988, p. 3). The possibility of greater wholeness, both emotionally and spiritually then seems within reach. This wholeness represents a striving towards psychological health, emotional freedom to be and spiritual life, where God is no longer a projection of a punitive parent but a 'loving God that enables Man to achieve His salvific purpose' (Meissner, 1984, p. 244).

Writing in such a way about these themes it seems as though there is a logical progression from the theme of sin to that of wholeness. However, that would be too simplistic, and there is no prescribed pathway along which this journey should be taken.

Discussion

The theme of sin, guilt, betrayal, doubt and wholeness concern the clergy not just on a religious level but also at a psychodynamic one. Though the word 'sin' is not part of the therapist's vocabulary, there is a prevailing view that there are 'human limits of a duality of human character – *good and evil* (Lovinger, 1984, p. 54). Implicit 'all-goodness' of people is not seen in the literature of Freud, Klein, and others. These authors see the seeds of discontent sown in the soil of early development, whereas the Christian see the human problem as originating in original sin. Within the Christian faith there is a striving after wholeness, a searching for growth and maturity.

Appendix 4: Questions to Bishops

1. What are the particular problems in the diocese?

2. What are the problems the clergy have to contend with?

3. Why do some clergy 'succeed' and others fail?

4. What support systems are in place?

5. Are they adequate? If not, how could they be improved?

6. How have women priests changed the Church in your diocese?

7. What is your role with your clergy?

8. How important are clergy family/spouses to you and to their work and what role should the diocese have with the spouse/family?

9. How much of a concern should the marital relationship of someone seeking ordination be to the Church?

10. Describe your thoughts about clergy marriage breakdown.

11. What more should the Church do about it?

12. What psychological reasons do you think may bring someone to seek ordination?

13. How do you cope when a priest loses their faith?

Appendix 5: Questions to the Director of the Ministry Division

1. Looking at the selection process, what are your feelings about it?

2. How could it be improved?

3. How has the ordination of women priests changed or affected the Church at large?

4. What other changes do you see happening?

5. How should the Church deal with inadequate clergy?

6. In the selection process and later on in their ministry, what role or importance do you see the clergy spouse or family taking?

7. What are your thoughts about clergy marriage breakdown?

Appendix 6: Questions to the Principal of the Theological College

1. What should be the aims and objectives of theological training?

2. Is that happening? If not, why not?

3 Where do you see the spouse/family of the ordinand fitting into all of this?

4. How concerned should selectors, DDOs, dioceses, bishops and yourself be about the marital relationship and how it will impact on the ministry?

5. What are the occasions when you prevent an ordinand going forward to ordination?

6. How receptive are bishops and dioceses to your negative evaluations of an ordinand?

7. How do you see the future of the Church of England?

8. Please give me your views of the state of clergy marriages and what the Church can do about it.

9. What psychological reasons do you think bring someone to seek ordination?

10. Emotional and spiritual health – what affects which? Is faith determined on a strong self-image or, if not, on what?

Bibliography

Atkinson, D. J. and Field, D. H. (1995)
The New Dictionary of Christian Ethics and Pastoral Theology, Inter-Varsity Press

Bowlby, J. (1973)
Attachment and Loss: Volume 2 – Separation, Anxiety and Anger, Penguin Books

Bowlby, J. (1979)
The Making and Breaking of Affectional Bonds, Tavistock Publications

Campbell, J. (1971)
The Portable, Penguin Books

Cambell, A. V. (1986)
Paid to Care: The limits of Professionals in Pastoral Care, SPCK

Chadwick, H (1991)
St Augustine' Confessions, Oxford University Press

Davie, G. (1994)
Religion in Britain since 1945, Blackwell

Deurzen-Smith, E. Van (1988)
Existential Counselling in Practise, Sage Publications

Dicks, H. V. (1967)
Marital Tensions, Routledge & Kegan Paul

Douglas, J. D., Hillyer, N, Bruce, F. F. and Guthrie, D., (1982)
New Bible Dictionary, Second Edition, Inter-Varsity Press

Dyer. A, (1990a)
Anvil, vol. 16, no. 2, Anvil Trust, Oxford.

Dyer, A. (1990b)
Paper prepared for the Rochester Bishop's Staff by the Department of Ministry and Training.

Dyer, A. (1999)
Reviewing the Reception: Five Years of Women Priests.

Eliot, T. S. (1963)
Collected Poems 1902-1962, Faber & Faber

Ferguson, S.B., and Wright, D.F., (1988)
New Dictionary of Theology, Inter-Varsity Press

Festinger, L. (1959)
A Theory of Cognitive Dissonance, Tavistock Publications

Foster, R. and Smith, J. B., (1993)
Devotional Classics, Hodder & Stoughton

Francis, L. J. and Jones S. H., (1996)
Psychological Perspectives on Christian Ministry, Gracewing

Freud, S., (1961)
The Future of an Illusion, Norton & Company

Freud, S., (1973)
New Introductory Lectures on Psychoanalysis, Penguin Books

Freud, S., (1977)
On Sexuality, Penguin Books

Freud, S., (1976)
Introductory Lectures on Psychoanalysis, Penguin Books

Hastings, A., (1987)
A History of English Christianity 1920-85, Collins Fount Paperbacks

Jacobs, M., (1986)
The Presenting Past, Harper & Row

Jung, C. G. (1968)
Analytical Psychology, Its Theory and Practice, Routledge & Kegan Paul

Kirk, M., & Leary, T., (1994)
Holy Matrimony? An exploration of Marriage and Ministry, Lynx

Leeder, L. (1977)
Ecclesiastical Law Handbook, Sweet & Maxwell.

Lovinger, R. (1984)
Working with Religious Issues in Therapy, Jason Aronson, Inc

Meissner, W. W. (1984)
Psychoanalysis and Religious Experience, Yale University Press

Ramsey, M. (1985)
The Christian Priest Today, SPCK

Rowe, D. (1983)
Depression. The Way out of Your Prison, London, Routledge & Kegan Paul

Russell, A. (1993)
The Country Parson, SPCK

Russell, A. (1980)
The Clerical Profession, SPCK

Rycroft, C. (1968)
A Critical Dictionary of Psychoanalysis, Penguin Books

Sinclair, Ferguson, B., and Wright D. F., (1988)
New Dictionary of Theology, Inter-Varsity Press

Skynner, A. C. R. (1976)
One Flesh Separate Persons – Principles of Family and Marital Psychotherapy, Constable

Spillius, E. B. (1989)
Melanie Klein Today, Routledge

Symington, N. (1993)
Narcissism. A New Theory, Karnac Books

The Alternative Service Book (1980), Hodder & Stoughton

Watts, F., and Williams, M. (1988)
The Psychology of Religious Knowing, Cambridge University Press

Winnicott, D. W. (1984)
The Maturational Process and the Facilitating Environment, Karnac Books

Winnicott, D. W. (1986)
Home Is Where We Start From, Penguin Books

Yalom, I. D. (1980)
Existential Psychotherapy, Basic Books